Praise for *Dynamically Different Classrooms*

Calling *all* teachers: this book will help you rethink your thinking and rejuvenate your learning strategies.

Dr Andy Cope, teacher, author and the UK's one and only doctor of happiness

There are plenty of books looking at the 'how' and 'what' of teaching, but not many ask us to consider the 'where'. In *Dynamically Different Classrooms*, however, Claire Gadsby and Jan Evans do exactly that as they share ideas and strategies that are underpinned by solid research and have been sourced from years of working with primary, middle and secondary schools across the UK to help create learning environments that enable every child to progress and thrive.

Does this mean spending endless hours constructing complex and beautiful wall displays, or spending non-existent funds on fancy furniture? Nope, the suggestions in this book are much smarter than that – supporting educators to rethink the space in which they teach, and make it work more effectively for them and their pupils.

Helen Mulley, Editor, *Teach Secondary*

Dynamically Different Classrooms combines learning theory with a range of practical strategies and shows how the classroom can be the arena to bring it all to life.

If we believe in active learning, this is a book to be acted upon.

Mick Waters, Professor of Education, University of Wolverhampton

Dynamically Different Classrooms breathes life into thinking creatively about teaching and learning. It is full not only of ideas proven to work, but also of methodological insights into *why* they work. Each chapter offers ideas about a different area of learning, often sharing powerful reminders that a fresh look at how we use our classroom space can make all the difference. It also provides a refreshing take on the holistic view of teaching the whole child, taking into account a consideration of emotional responses.

This book will be fantastically useful for primary and secondary school teachers alike – and I believe every parent in the land would want their child to have the kind of learning experience that it champions, where the importance is placed on creativity, resilience and curiosity rather than on exam results alone.

Rachel Jones, teacher, King Edward VI School, author of *Teacher Geek* and curator of *Don't Change the Light Bulbs*

In an educational landscape where different trends and fads come and go, *Dynamically Different Classrooms* is filled with the wisdom that only experience can bring. The main messages from recent and robust research are all put in one place and told through an array of creative examples and practical strategies, which makes this book a treasure trove of inspiration and ideas!

Chris Martin, Principal, St Thomas Aquinas Catholic Secondary School

It is no surprise to me that Claire Gadsby and Jan Evans would produce a book that communicates such energy and excitement in both content and tone. We have benefitted as a school from Jan's wealth of experience in developing active engagement in children through higher-order questioning, and we shall certainly 'magpie' from the wonderful variety of ideas presented here. As ever, Claire and Jan's passion is infectious – and it is refreshing to come across a book that leaves the reader feeling so energised.

Clare Smith, Head Teacher, St Joseph's Catholic Primary School

CREATE SPACES
THAT SPARK LEARNING

DYNAMICALLY
DIFFERENT

CLASSROOMS CLAIRE GADSBY & JAN EVANS

independent
thinking pr

First published by

Independent Thinking Press
Crown Buildings, Bancyfelin, Carmarthen, Wales, SA33 5ND, UK
www.independentthinkingpress.com

and

Independent Thinking Press
PO Box 2223, Williston, VT 05495, USA
www.crownhousepublishing.com

Independent Thinking Press is an imprint of Crown House Publishing Ltd.

British Library Cataloguing-in-Publication Data

A catalogue entry for this book is available from the British Library.

Print ISBN 978-178135297-7
Mobi ISBN 978-178135318-9
ePub ISBN 978-178135319-6
ePDF ISBN 978-178135323-3

LCCN 2019932886

Printed and bound in the UK by
Gomer Press, Llandysul, Ceredigion

Claire:

For my precious daughter Poppy Matilda who brings joy, always.

And for my dear friend and mentor Annabel Luery, who first showed me what great teaching looks like and who inspires me to this day.

Jan:

For Laura and David – I am always so proud of you both.

And for Teddy Albert – may your learning journey be exciting and fun.

ACKNOWLEDGEMENTS

Thank you to all the teachers, teaching assistants and pupils who have always made us feel so welcome in their classrooms. Your willingness, enthusiasm and creativity have been a constant source of inspiration. We literally could not have written this book without you.

Jane, our wonderful photographer and friend, thank you for bringing the ideas to life. You instantly 'got' what we wanted to do and set about capturing some truly moving classroom moments as photos that we never tire of looking at.

Many thanks to Ian Gilbert for challenging our thinking and for steering us in the right direction. Your insight and advice was invaluable.

Our heartfelt thanks go to the whole team at Independent Thinking Press who listened to our original ideas and who have been incredibly patient and reassuring as this book has evolved.

Special thanks must go to our amazing editor, Louise. You have encouraged us and shown incredible patience, tact and understanding. Your attention to detail is amazing and you have been so in tune with our thinking that it has felt very much a joint effort. As the saying goes: 'you have gone above and beyond …'

Finally, thank you from the bottom of our hearts to our long-suffering partners, Kevin and Bob. For all your love, patience and support throughout the process of writing this book.

Claire:

Kevin, thank you for all your love and support. I couldn't do any of this without you.

Jan:

Bob, you are my rock, always.

CONTENTS

INTRODUCTION

Imagine a classroom where every display invites an active pupil response. Where learning clues fall from the ceiling. Where the floors feature challenges. Welcome to the world of dynamically different classrooms.

As education consultants we have worked with thousands of teachers over the years and a great deal of our time has been spent developing techniques to help pupils become autonomous learners who are actively engaged and confident in their learning, and able to transfer and apply it at different times and in different contexts. All too often, though, we felt that teachers were overlooking a key element in their practice: namely the contribution that their physical classroom environment could make to learning.

Over three years, we have had the privilege of working with primary, middle, secondary and special schools across the UK, exploring the untapped potential of their classrooms. This action research evolved to become the Dynamically Different Classroom Project and has directly informed this book. We have developed and refined the suggested techniques through our coaching work with teachers and, whilst we know that you may already be using some of these ideas, we hope that we offer an abundance of new ones to try.

I had never really considered the impact of a well-constructed display. I had only ever been taught that they should look lovely, and maybe have some keywords for the children to use. However, the Dynamically Different Classroom training genuinely transformed my practice. I no longer create displays prior to learning: the display is our learning. We ask questions; we try to answer them; we evidence our learning and share the journey week by week through photographs, video links and sticky notes. Displays shouldn't be symmetrical boards that look good on Pinterest or Instagram: they should be purposeful and should support learning. Following the training, I hope that mine are. However, I know that mastering the art of a dynamically different classroom is an ongoing process, and I am incredibly excited to continue to trial many more of Claire and Jan's ideas to aid the teaching and learning in my classroom.

Rosie, Hoyland Common Primary

So what do we mean by 'dynamically different'?

The term 'dynamic' is synonymous with:

❯ Continuous change or progress.

❯ Activity and vigour.

❯ Powerful energy.

❯ Effective action.

These are the very ideas that define the spirit of the dynamically different classroom: a space where engagement and movement are expected, and displays and the environment constantly evolve.

We are keen for teachers to re-examine the dynamics of their own classroom in order to establish an optimum, positive atmosphere where pupils feel comfortable communicating with each other and with their teacher. Investing time and energy in developing this kind of connected classroom, where pupils perceive each other as allies and not judges, is crucial for the development of metacognitive, confident learners.

From captives to captivated

A 'standard' primary classroom, built for 30 pupils, should be at least 56 m^2, although 70 m^2 is recommended to allow flexible use and wheelchair access (Department for Education and Skills, 2005: 31). Guidelines for secondary schools consider a similar space to be standard for 30 pupils, at 60 m^2 (Department for Education and Skills, 2004: 34). Pupils are essentially captive in these small classrooms for, according to our calculations, approximately 10,500 hours of their young lives, at a time when they are least equipped to deal with such physical constraint.

Movement is advocated strongly throughout this book for a variety of reasons. Not only does it seem common sense to punctuate those hours of classroom containment with regular physical movement, there is also a wealth of scientific evidence attesting to the link between movement and learning:

> *We know exercise fuels the brain with oxygen, but it also feeds it neurotropins (high-nutrient chemical 'packages') to increase the number of connections between neurons. Most astonishingly, exercise is known to increase the baseline of new neuron growth. Rats grow more brain cells when they exercise than when they don't exercise (Van Praag et al., 1999). In addition, studies link this increased neurogenesis to increased cognition, better memory, and reduced likelihood of depression (Kempermann, 2002).*

(Jensen, 2005: 63)

Jensen (2005: 66) goes on to say that simply incorporating movement into routine classroom activities would re-energise pupils and fuel their brains with oxygen and that, 'Teachers who insist that students remain seated during the entire class period are not promoting optimal conditions for learning.'

However, although the value of using movement within learning experiences is becoming increasingly acknowledged, it can feel uncomfortable. Some teachers find it difficult to know how to incorporate this, especially as pupils get older and physically larger.

Rather than suppressing youngsters' energy and desire for movement, we have set out to deliberately harness this with many of the techniques, to further boost both engagement and retention. Keeping young people active, engaged and healthy in the physical environment where they spend the majority of their waking hours should be a top priority for all teachers.

We cannot magically make our classrooms bigger, but incorporating movement into lessons does not actually require a massive area. In this book, we explore how you can allow every pupil to experience the finite classroom space in an almost infinite number of ways.

At Westwood, we make use of every surface: the ceilings, floors, windows and walls are all used to engage our children and we encourage them not to be restricted to writing in exercise books – this sees them choosing to write on the tables, windows or on sugar paper. It is normal to see children laying on their tummies on the floor or curled up in a comfy chair to complete their work.

Lauraine, Westwood Primary School

Teachers often comment on a sense of 'initiative overload' when exposed to new ideas about practice, compounded by insufficient time to dive beneath the surface to explore where and how the underlying principles connect. What we've tried to do in this book is to distil some of the main messages from recent, robust research about the role of the environment in children's learning and produce a range of practical techniques that you can use to maximise the potential of your classroom. We invite you to focus on common features at the heart of any effective pedagogical approach and then to harness your own creativity to make full use of your physical learning environment.

The merits, or otherwise, of various methods of curriculum delivery are always the subject of much debate in education and, like Agatha Christie's play *The Mousetrap*, will probably continue to 'run and run'. There has always been a danger of creating an extreme 'pendulum swing' approach with pedagogical styles when, as with most things, a varied and balanced approach is generally best. As the teacher, only you know your current pupils' individual needs, and only you will know when it is more appropriate to incorporate different elements – such as whole-class teaching, inquiry-based group work, individual project work, etc. Your classroom's physical environment is both a reflection of and a delivery agent for your pedagogical approach.

The classroom environment has recently been subject to some extreme, alternative approaches, as demonstrated on social media, where people have posted images of their newly stripped back, minimalist classrooms along with accounts of how they have exchanged their brightly coloured display boards for plain white ones. Overstimulation for pupils – especially for those with special educational needs and disabilities (SEND) – caused by crammed, colourful walls is often cited as the main reason for this. However, a study by the University of Salford, conducted with primary school children, showed that when a carefully thought out physical environment considered the elements of stimulation, individualisation and naturalness, it could have a significant impact on academic achievement:

> Differences in the physical characteristics of classrooms explain 16% of the variation in learning progress over a year for the 3766 pupils included in the study. Or to make this more tangible, it is estimated that the impact of moving an 'average' child from the least effective to the most effective space would be around 1.3 sub-levels, a big impact when pupils typically make 2 sub-levels progress a year.
>
> **(Barrett et al., 2015: 3)**

Particularly relevant is that when looking at the influence of visual stimulation in the classroom, the report findings showed a curvilinear effect, with high or low levels of complexity producing poorer learning conditions (Barrett et al., 2015: 34). In other words, the 'Goldilocks' alternative of a 'just right', intermediate level had the greatest impact on pupils' learning. The National Association of Special Educational Needs (nasen) also highlighted the role a well-resourced classroom could play, especially in reducing pressure on working memory (nasen, 2015: 7).

As noted previously, only you really know the make-up of your pupils and, obviously, you have to be very mindful of their individual needs whilst still promoting an inclusive approach. Chapter 2 contains a case study of a Year 8 nurture group which demonstrates how this can be achieved. The teacher, Amie, wanted to incorporate some techniques that could have been very overwhelming for particular pupils. However, she discussed the planned activities with them and together they formulated a way to proceed. The resulting lesson was very successful and the pupils' sustained engagement, and the impact on their learning, was obvious for all to see. The techniques in this book aim to give you a repertoire of ideas to make your classroom environment purposeful, provocative and engaging whilst striking the appropriate balance in terms of stimulation.

A systematic review of evidence across all phases of education, commissioned by Education Scotland, identified the most effective learning environments and conditions for the development of creative thinking and problem-solving skills (Davies et al., 2013). The report concluded that the findings concerning the impact of environment on pupils' attainment, and the resulting policy recommendations, have implications for all teachers. Recommendations included having classrooms that can be used flexibly and allow the movement of pupils around different areas to support the growth of their ideas. The report also found evidence about the value of incorporating an element of novelty and pupil choice into the classroom.

All of these elements are strongly promoted throughout the following chapters and the techniques are designed to provide some novel ways to support you in the development of these aspects of your pedagogical approach.

Of all the approaches which focus on the significance of the classroom environment, perhaps one of the most well-known is Reggio Emilia. Although arising originally from the pre-school and primary phases of education, its fundamental ideas about the settings in which children learn have relevance for all stages. The Reggio Emilia philosophy talks about three educators being in the classroom at any one time: the teacher, the child and the environment. This approach stresses the role of the environment as the 'third teacher' in the total, interactive educational experience (Robson and Mastrangelo, 2017).

Thinking of the environment in this way sets up the expectation that pupils will interact with it. Therefore, there is an implied responsibility on the part of the teacher to do their utmost to ensure that the physical environment promotes and supports active engagement.

Your classroom is your domain and it can be difficult to look at it afresh and break away from old habits and routines. However, by considering the environment as the third teacher, and by questioning your present use of it, you can begin to notice how your surroundings can become a truly dynamic space that contributes to children's learning.

Next steps

The vast majority of the techniques in this book can be adapted to use with all age groups. Whilst some ideas may seem to fit more naturally with primary or secondary, we would urge you not to dismiss the more experimental and active techniques as suitable for younger learners only. We have seen some very creative approaches work with older pupils, where teachers have adopted a tongue-in-cheek attitude and played on their adolescent, ironic sense of humour.

Research tells us that we have a rising tide of mental health issues amongst our young people. They are more stressed, insular and depressed today than ever before, with the pressure of exams often cited as a particular concern for teenagers:

> *An alarming number of young people feel paralysed by their circumstances and crippling self-doubt. More than a quarter (28 per cent) do not feel in control of their lives and 16 per cent go as far as to say they think their life will amount to nothing, no matter how hard they try. Many young people feel trapped by their circumstances, with almost a fifth (18 per cent)*

stating that they do not have the ability to change their circumstances if they want to.

(The Prince's Trust, 2017: 14)

Throughout the pilot phase of the Dynamically Different Classroom Project, we were continually struck by the positive impact of the more innovative, physical techniques on older learners. Watching GCSE pupils work together to unleash learning-link paper chains from the ceiling (see Chapter 2) or lie shoulder to shoulder to complete whole-class learning scrolls (see Chapter 3) was fascinating.

At a stage in their lives when pupils are besieged by all that adolescence involves, these techniques brought a little lightness and playfulness back. Yes, we saw surprise when we asked pupils to lie down on the floor, and got more than a few odd looks when paper plates were introduced as Tasty Tacos (see Chapter 2), but after the initial typical teenage cynicism, we witnessed genuine curiosity and engagement. We saw pupils relaxing into collaborative working. We saw them laughing and chatting about the work. We saw memorable learning happening precisely because it was unusual and collaborative. We saw young people enjoying learning. Ultimately, your own professional knowledge and creativity are the only 'limiters' as to how, when and where these techniques can be tweaked and put to good use.

Working smarter

We estimate that the average teacher will deliver more than 20,000 lessons during a 30-year career and, as a well-worn adage states, 'If you always do what you've always done, you'll always get what you've always got.' We are keen for teachers to work smarter, not harder, and to explore the cumulative effect of marginal gains: those tiny little tweaks to existing good practice which, when added together, can lead to dynamic shifts and improved outcomes for pupils.

One aspect of working smarter when thinking about how the learning will unfold involves teachers redirecting their creative energy into designing the infrastructure of the classroom. This would mark the end of the anonymous learning space and provide a real opportunity for teachers to make bold, customised choices, not merely in terms of fixtures, fittings and aesthetics, but in terms of the more fundamental beliefs they have as educators.

The physicality of a dynamically different classroom operates as an active teaching tool, boosting both engagement and progress. Consider the following quick tweaks:

❭ Any existing display can be quickly adapted and made more interactive and engaging by being used as a memory aid, team competition or 'spot the red herring' style challenge (see Chapter 1).

❭ Any ceiling can be used as a virtual 'cloud storage' system where current learning is deposited (perhaps as learning-link paper chains), before being reintroduced when the pupils least expect it (see Chapter 2).

❯ Any floor can be repurposed to form a 'circuit training' lesson, with stepping stone challenges between each station (see Chapter 3).

❯ Any corner can be used dynamically to target different learning outcomes – for example, the teacher could offer differentiated support by modelling a task and inviting pupils to Magpie Me (see Chapter 4).

The fundamental premise is that there is nothing static within this kind of classroom: everything is kept 'simmering', ready to turn up the learning heat. Once the space is set up, a teacher can very easily redirect and refresh the learning merely by using the infrastructure itself as a dynamic learning tool. Time invested in maximising the classroom's potential influence on pupil outcomes will never be time wasted.

It was interesting to hear from teachers involved in the pilot of the Dynamically Different Classroom Project about the immediate impact that they saw after incorporating some of the techniques. Generally, they said:

❯ They were impressed by the way in which pupils responded to the techniques and the sustained level of engagement.

❯ They felt that high-quality learning was generated but that minimal input from them had been required during the actual lessons.

❯ They felt they had been able to circulate more freely and therefore able to respond to the needs and interests of specific groups and individuals more effectively.

❯ They were genuinely impressed with the nature and quality of the discussions generated and saw pupils expressing their ideas with greater confidence.

❯ They were surprised by the way in which pupils easily assumed responsibility and started to direct their own learning.

❯ They felt that pupils had shown greater curiosity and demonstrated more satisfaction with their learning.

❯ They felt that their teaching had been refreshed and they felt energised, wanting to carry on trying out new approaches.

It may also be comforting to teachers in this current climate of accountability to remember that when pupils become advocates of their own learning – and demonstrate this in explicit, audible and highly visible ways – the evidence of their progress becomes incontrovertible.

Many of the teachers initially involved in the project decided to start implementing techniques by focusing on separate areas of their classrooms. However, some decided that they wanted to adopt a more holistic approach and follow a themed focus across the environment.

To accommodate both preferences we have taken six key themes and cross-referenced each of the techniques to one of them. (Although, obviously, we appreciate that many of the techniques will address more than one theme.) You can use this colour-coding to navigate your own pathway through the chapters according to your development priorities.

Our six themes are:

1. Metacognition and self-regulated learning

Metacognition describes pupils' ability to monitor, direct and review their learning. Effective metacognitive strategies get learners to think about their own learning more explicitly. Teaching them to set goals – and monitor and evaluate their own academic progress and challenges – is a key part of this process, with an Education Endowment Foundation (EEF) report recommending that we should, 'Set an appropriate level of challenge to develop pupils' self-regulation and metacognition' (Quigley, Muijs and Stringer, 2018: 18).

Whilst these skills are undoubtedly important, they are also tricky to cultivate. We want our pupils to be risk takers: to be unafraid to try and to fail. However, young people receive conflicting messages. 'Be careful,' say their worried parents whilst the world is crying out for resilient characters who are happy to take risks and develop entrepreneurial spirits by daring to try new things and by growing through failures. Whilst motivational posters, assemblies and visiting speakers are commonplace in schools, what can be done to move away from the rhetoric and change actual practice?

Psychology reminds us that people can experience exactly the same stimulus or event, such as riding on a roller coaster, but have completely different responses to it. The key difference rests on whether we perceive it as a threat or an opportunity (Busch and Watson, 2017: 42). People are able to reframe their perceptions and this skill can be explicitly taught to pupils by using language such as, 'Although this may feel stressful, this is an opportunity to …'

We need to ensure that all lessons are sufficiently challenging so that each pupil routinely has to explore, clarify and refine their conceptual understanding. We want them to be excited about not being sure yet and about the prospect of trying to become surer. This process of finding your own way out of uncertainty is what James Nottingham refers to as being in the 'learning pit'.[1]

Hopefully we are all familiar with the definite, physical and positive feeling we get when we've mastered a challenge that moved us out of our comfort zone (and with the almost involuntary fist-pump gesture that often accompanies these

---

1 See https://www.jamesnottingham.co.uk/learning-pit/.

successes). Nothing is as energising or engaging as working at the very edge of your ability. When you are truly 'in the zone' or in a 'state of flow', you want to stay there; quitting is an unsatisfactory outcome (Csikszentmihalyi, 2002). Designing lessons that have appropriate, differentiated levels of challenge for our pupils is a major component of engaging them emotionally.

To genuinely improve learning, lessons may well need to be more difficult. Sometimes, as teachers, we make things too easy and too comfortable – and this, in turn, can convey low expectations. Indeed, one of the key recommendations from boys' achievement expert Gary Wilson (2013: 1) is to stop doing everything for them.

We now invite you to think about which physical elements you could introduce as aids to pupils' self-sufficiency that will empower them as truly autonomous leaders of their own learning. Many teachers will already be developing the growth mindsets of their learners through everyday activities, such as promoting a culture of 'no single right answer', or by making deliberate mistakes themselves. Some teachers will be taking this further by making their pupils aware of the work of researchers like Carol Dweck (2017), and planning sets of lessons about brain neuroplasticity, with activities such as making thinking caps to show the functions of the different brain areas. By highlighting skills that pupils have learned over time and encouraging them to learn a new one, such as juggling, they can understand the 'plastic' nature of their brain. This goes a long way towards helping pupils realise that they can grow their own intelligence. However, we believe there is untapped potential in the physical environment of the classroom, which we can better exploit.

The environment itself needs to be facilitative in order to support pupils' resilience. Maximum effects are derived from high levels of challenge but with access to high levels of appropriate support (Fletcher and Sarkar, 2016).

An appropriate classroom ethos, with high expectations in terms of thoroughness and quality, helps to build stamina and resilience when we employ strategies that:

❯ Allow pupils to select and use supporting resources independently.

❯ Give access to clear success criteria and quality models, with the intention that pupils achieve this standard in their work.

❯ Allow pupils to understand the value of talk as a tool for thinking and learning.

❯ Provide pupils with opportunities to give oral presentations to a variety of audiences.

❯ Provide opportunities for pupils to engage in speculative, exploratory and reciprocal discussions and refine their understanding as a result.

❯ Encourage reflective self-evaluation about their emotional response to challenging activities.

> Activate pupils as people involved in helping each other learn.

> Involve pupils in the design and co-construction of future learning.

> Promote and nurture inspiration and aspiration.

> Nurture pupils' appreciation of the power of iteration.

> Help all pupils to develop and sustain a capacity to learn that lasts not only through the years of compulsory schooling but benefits them throughout their lives.

Pupils can be infinitely resourceful if they are given an appropriate support system. Several years ago we were told a story by an experienced secondary school colleague that illustrates this brilliantly. She had recently returned from teaching abroad and was working as a supply teacher whilst looking for a permanent appointment. On one occasion she had, rather reluctantly, accepted a request to cover a class of 5-year-olds. She described how she entered a chaotic scene of small children noisily moving around and constantly needing help and attention. One pupil (who was obviously very astute for his age) eventually came up to her and, using phraseology obviously cultivated by their regular teacher, said, 'Miss, when *real* miss gets harassed, she puts on the scarf [indicating a pashmina on the back of the teacher's chair] and we all go into independent learning mode.' She picked up the scarf and as soon as some of the pupils saw this there was some frantic whispering as they got into groups, put their folders on their desks and gathered resource trays from the side of the room before settling down to work collaboratively on some quite challenging activities, without approaching the teacher at all. We loved the story; it just goes to show how self-reliant even very young learners can be when familiar with classroom routines and high expectations.

Carefully orchestrated choices work hand in hand with challenge to support the development of resilience. Whilst some teachers may be uncomfortable with the idea of too much

● Metacognition and self-regulated learning | Emotional engagement ▲ Retrieval and revision

choice, in Daniel Pink's influential book *Drive* (2010: 204) research on motivation and resilience places autonomy at the top of a list of three motivating factors:

1   '*Autonomy*—The desire to direct our own lives'. Be aware that too much choice can be a problem, especially for younger children, and so it may be sensible to begin with fixed/limited choices.

2   '*Mastery*—The urge to get better and better at something that matters'. The emphasis here should be upon improving your own personal best, and we should educate young people about the danger of comparing yourself to others. This can be a particular challenge for today's youth, who are so heavily influenced by social media and comparisons to each other.

3   '*Purpose*—The yearning to do what we do in the service of something larger than ourselves'. It may also be helpful to demonstrate how the learning connects directly to the aspirations and future aims of our young people.

The picture described here may well require teachers to shift their view of their relationship with their learners to a 'partnering' one. We have often seen this described as being a 'facilitator'; however, we have reservations about the connotations of that term. Rather than being someone who 'makes a difficult process easier', as the definition suggests, we see you using your skills and knowledge to be the overall *driving* partner. A partnering role sees the teacher providing structure and support; constantly assessing and adjusting the learning environment to provide appropriately differentiated challenges, and creative opportunities, for the pupils in their quest for resilience and autonomous learning. It's well worth reading Marc Prensky's *Teaching Digital Natives* (2010), as this takes the concept of partnering even further and looks at ways to develop an effective pedagogy for 21st century learners.

2. Emotional engagement

'People will forget what you say and forget what you do, but they will never forget how you made them feel.'

Attributed to Maya Angelou

I've come to realise that teaching and learning is at its best when you feel something. The first Dynamically Different Classroom Project meeting opened with this quote attributed to the inspirational Maya Angelou that really resonates with me now, and has done so on several occasions throughout my professional career and personal experiences. I suppose that this quote has become my mantra. I repeatedly come back to it. I want learners to feel something when they are in my lessons: from being stretched by challenge or curiosity to awe and wonder stuff.

Amie, Darton College

This whole book is based upon the principle of active engagement and we invite you to think further about what it means for learning to be truly 'irresistible': in other words, where the environment is so compelling that even would-be reluctant pupils can be hooked in. We want to explore how the very atmosphere of the classroom can be cultivated and deliberately used to ensure pupils' active participation and immersed engagement in their learning potential.

The idea of an 'irresistible' learning space may conjure up images of large-scale artworks or attractive installations and, certainly, these could contribute to a feeling of awe and wonder. Many schools already go even further by literally transforming their classrooms and communal spaces into somewhere else – for example, we've seen a reconstruction of Tutankhamun's tomb, a library converted into the 'Olde Curiosity Shoppe' and a corridor turned into a First World War trench.

However, for us, the notion goes much deeper than this. We know that atmosphere is vitally important to learning. If we challenged you now to close your eyes, imagine yourself back in your own school days and think of a time when you were totally engaged, chances are you would recall something of the feel of the experience – as learning itself is a sensory experience (see Stafford, 2012).

So we know that the atmosphere of the classroom is important, but it's also necessary to make sure this doesn't become too familiar or predictable. By introducing unexpected elements into our lessons, we begin to intrigue our learners. Add

to this the fact that curious learners tend to be more motivated and effective and it is clear that to make learning experiences 'irresistible' we need to harness these elements. In other words, as teachers, we should be doing all we can to exploit variety and novelty and create an atmosphere of awe and wonder.

We want all our pupils to be engrossed: for their classrooms to be places where they experience a sense of purpose, challenge and achievement. Our experience as educators tells us that learners who are having fun and are engaged in the learning process are more likely to better retain and recall the content, but, obviously, do beware of 'fun' simply for its own sake. The stakes, in terms of learners' life chances, are simply too high for us to get swept up in novelty if there is no impact on learning. We need to ensure that lessons are a blend of high challenge and high support – and this book demonstrates how to exploit the physical environment as a major part of that strategy.

Providing the right level of support is important. However, teachers often comment that they seem to be working harder than their pupils, and another common concern relates to the short attention spans of today's learners and how difficult it can be to engage them. There's no doubt that our pupils are part of the 'born digital' generation (Prensky, 2010). In other words, they have grown up in an age in which receiving, gathering, retaining and applying information in highly interactive ways is the norm. So surely our lesson delivery needs to reflect this? We need to

⬤ Metacognition and self-regulated learning | Emotional engagement ▲ Retrieval and revision

employ strategies and techniques that emulate their world rather than simply hoping that we can capture and retain our pupils' interest through a reliance on more 'traditional' approaches.

One such example could be presenting learning as game-like activities, through which pupils start to intuitively understand the incremental and cumulative nature of learning. They engage in the process and they become motivated to keep working towards the next level up and the eventual end goal. The incentives are demonstrating mastery and engaging with further challenges, rather than merely finishing their work. Pupils of all ages also engage more readily with something if they can see the relevance or real-life application of it. Helping pupils to see the value and transferability of skills that they are developing goes a long way towards off-setting disengagement.

As a final piece of inspiration, do take a look at the very powerful strategies in *Uncharted Territories: Adventures in Learning* by Hywel Roberts and Debra Kidd (2018). It is packed with hooks into exploratory learning that place learners of whatever age knee-deep in dilemma, encouraging deep, analytical and imaginative thinking.

The key idea in this theme is that emotional investment – nurtured by a sense of surprise, intrigue and, of course, supportive challenge and accomplishment – helps to lay a firm foundation for subsequent learning. It is also important that this process allows learners to experience success. In seeing evidence of their acheivements, a strong, positive sense of their own ability is mirrored back, and this nurtures pupils' resilience.

▲ 3. Retrieval and revision

The work of Robert Bjork, one of the world's leading experts on learning and memory, highlights the distinction between performance and true, long-term learning:

> *That performance is often fleeting and, consequently, a highly imperfect index of learning does not appear to be appreciated by learners or instructors who frequently misinterpret short-term performance as a guide to long-term learning.*

(Soderstrom and Bjork, 2013)

Clearly, in a culture of linear examinations we have to pay particular attention to the conditions that will support deep, long-term learning and mastery. Bjork notes that there are, in fact, certain conditions that could appear to impede performance during training but that actually yield greater long-term benefits; these are 'desirable difficulties'.[2] By using the classroom environment to cultivate these conditions, we can exploit its potential to help pupils learn more.

Bjork's desirable difficulties inform many of the techniques in this book and include:

> **Spacing:** This is the finding that when information is spread out and repeated over periods of time it is learned more effectively than when it is studied in blocks with no intervals.

> **The New Theory of Disuse:** Bjork's theory found that by increasing the periods of time between practices we can make learning yet more effective, as we are making the information less accessible and therefore more challenging.

> **Generation:** This involves pupils generating words from memory or from clues instead of merely reading them. This could involve presenting keywords as anagrams or providing pupils with only the first letter or two to support their recall.

> **Testing:** This has been shown to be more effective than simply relearning the same material over and over again. Tests should be low stakes and low threat. For example, this could take the form of quizzes, self-testing, and generating questions to pair with answers.

> **Varying:** Even within one topic, vary the mode and conditions of the learning. This means ensuring that information is presented to and processed by pupils in many different ways.

> **Interleaving:** Pupils have many different things to learn and interleaving has a powerful role to play in helping them do this effectively. For instance, in a primary school context, this could involve a brief multiple-choice quiz on the Egyptians, followed immediately by maths problem solving, then a 'fill in the blanks' recap of the class reading. At secondary stage, you might alternate between different topics in a similar way.

---

2 See https://bjorklab.psych.ucla.edu/research/.

For example, in English, you could begin the lesson with a 'true or false' quiz based on poetry, followed by annotating extracts from a different set text in the main part of the lesson, then a 'fill in the blanks' grammar-related plenary.

The practical techniques in this book can be used to develop deep learning as well as records of that learning which can be easily accessed for frequent revision. We are advocating a more dynamic, innovative and active approach to revision generally: an energy we hope we have captured in the phrase 'retrieval and revision'.

4. Responsive teaching: using formative assessment to support the progress of *all* pupils, including vulnerable groups

The research evidence suggests that when formative assessment practices are integrated into the minute-to-minute and day-by-day classroom activities of teachers, substantial increases in student achievement—of the order of a 70 to 80 percent increase in the speed of learning—are possible, even when outcomes are measured with externally-mandated standardized tests.

(Leahy and Wiliam, 2009: 15)

Formative assessment is not new. Dylan Wiliam and Paul Black's seminal *Inside the Black Box* was published way back in 1990 and many schools have engaged with formative assessment, at least on some level, in the intervening years. Is your assessment practice based on habits and routines that have become formulaic? We have seen first-hand how the practical and highly engaging activities we share here can help to refresh and repurpose existing assessment practices.

Assessment for learning (AfL) is defined as:

part of everyday practice by students, teachers and peers that seeks, reflects upon and responds to information from dialogue, demonstration and observation in ways that enhance ongoing learning.

(AFL, 2009: 2)

Much of this is rather harder in practice than in theory. Teachers typically comment that whilst a lot of time and energy is spent 'seeking' assessment data, it is more challenging to find adequate time for the crucial business of reflecting on and responding to that information. It is clear that a responsive classroom lies at the very heart of successful formative assessment and is characterised by what Dylan Wiliam (2006: 11) describes as pedagogies of engagement and contingency.

The really important thing is that you create challenging learning environments—'high nutrition' environments to make students smarter, but if we look at the typical classroom it is clear some students participate and some students don't. [...] So because environment creates intelligence and intelligence creates environment, what we have to do is to create classrooms which are inclusive, where the level of cognitive demand is high, and where participation is obligatory.

(Wiliam, 2006: 6)

The term 'responsive teaching' has been suggested as an alternative name for formative assessment, and it may be timely to consider how responsive your own school and classroom are. For instance, is there capacity to regroup pupils easily? Can you work with smaller groups within your classroom whenever necessary? Or does the layout of your classroom mean that pupil groupings and working routines are quite stubbornly fixed?

Does the classroom enable you to respond to pupils who need extra support, without distracting or derailing the rest of the class? As teachers, we know what the knottiest, most difficult aspects of the curriculum are. By planning with these at the forefront of our minds, we can be much more strategic and ready to offer appropriate support. Why not try introducing mechanisms that allow you, the teacher and

lead pedagogue, to work more closely with the learners who need you the most? For example, by basing yourself in a zone within the classroom where they can go for additional help.

Feedback is a key element of formative assessment and responsive teaching, and the best kind can have a powerful impact on pupils' learning. According to the EEF, one evaluation of AfL indicated an impact of half of a GCSE grade per student per subject is achievable, which would be in line with the wider evidence about feedback.[3] However, as many teachers will no doubt agree, making feedback work

---

3 See https://educationendowmentfoundation.org.uk/evidence-summaries/teaching-learning-toolkit/feedback/.

effectively for every child in their classroom is difficult. Many are still investing huge amounts of time and energy into feedback practices that are exhausting and yet have negligible impact. The practical approaches throughout this book aim to correct this by helping teachers to identify where specific misconceptions lie, or where learning has not yet transferred into pupils' long-term memory. When pupils stand next to an incorrect answer as part of a Go and Stand (GAS) activity (see Chapter 3) or struggle with a particular Stepping Stone (also Chapter 3), we can immediately see the misunderstanding and begin to deliver specific feedback more effectively. Strategies involving zoned areas, such as the Helpful Huddle and Secret Challenge (see Chapter 4), are particularly effective tools for allowing teachers to work directly with pupils who need extra support to unpick misunderstandings and misconceptions.

5. Oracy and 'word wealth'

Words are powerful. They are the makers of meaning and are crucial in allowing us to understand the world and then to verbalise that understanding. Some studies indicate that having a restricted vocabulary as a young child is associated with poorer outcomes later on, as noted by Alex Quigley (2018: 3–4), who summarises research by Horowitz and Samuels suggesting that children from professional families hear their parents speak 32 million more words by the age of four than their counterparts in families claiming welfare.

These reported gaps don't end with childhood. Many studies have been undertaken which show a strong correlation between poor vocabulary skills at 5 years old and poor reading skills, higher levels of unemployment and even poor mental health in adulthood (Quigley, 2018: 6). In school, many of the challenges presented by the current national curriculum in England are due, at least in part, to its emphasis on complex academic vocabulary and increased expectations for reading comprehension. GCSEs are also considerably harder and, according to Quigley (2018: 13), 'At every year of secondary school, children are routinely reading texts that are considerably beyond their chronological age.'

Despite these challenges, and the purported vocabulary gap, too little has been done in terms of explicit vocabulary teaching, with Quigley (2018: 19) claiming that 'conscious, deliberate attention to word learning is necessary if we are to give every child access to the academic code needed for school success'. Quigley (2018: 2) describes a 'word-hoard of 50,000 words' as being necessary for every child to thrive in school and beyond.

Whilst some more recent studies have disputed the idea of a vocabulary gap based on economic status, we can surely safely conclude that all children will benefit from repeated opportunities to engage with language (Bower: 2018). As such, this book abounds with practical ideas for how to develop what Quigley (2018: 144) terms a 'word rich' classroom. Consider for a moment the sheer amount of vocabulary your learners are expected to use. For example, do our young learners know a triangle from a square and a clause from a conjunction? Leaping ahead a few years to GCSE science, can learners distinguish 'reproducibility' from 'variability'? Can they recall these terms in highly stressful exam situations, as well as decoding the challenging and precise wording of the questions? For many, sadly, the answer is no.

Our learners are confronted by a mind-blowing array of terminology at every stage of their schooling and we cannot rely on the assumption that they are absorbing this, osmosis-like, and automatically transferring it into their long-term memory. Instead, it behoves us to utilise a range of strategies that go beyond traditional glossaries and build active engagement with vocabulary, whilst also drawing upon what we now know about how memory works. Again, Bjork's principles of spacing learning and varying the conditions of practice underpin many of the stimulating activities that develop this theme.

Moving beyond vocabulary alone, there is a well-recognised link between talk and cognitive development. It is through vibrant and structured dialogue that learners can work collaboratively and begin to enjoy the sense of learning in an active away:

Children directly taught how to talk to others are better able to access the education on offer in class, and better able to listen to and shape their own thoughts.

(Dawes, 2018)

For many years, experts have recommended dialogic talk in classrooms. Dialogic talk is described by Neil Mercer (2003: 74) as 'that in which both teachers and pupils make substantial and significant contributions and through which pupils' thinking on a given idea or theme is helped to move forward.' Strategies which promote this kind of collaborative talk run throughout this book.

Kate Nation, professor of experimental psychology at the University of Oxford, said that language variation in children was complex and difficult to attribute to a single cause.

'Regardless of the causes, low levels of vocabulary set limits on literacy, understanding, learning the curriculum and can create a downward spiral of poor language which begins to affect all aspects of life,' Nation said.

(Adams, 2018)

Looking beyond the school years, oracy is a key component of overall literacy, which in itself is key to greater social mobility and improved life chances for all, including our most vulnerable learners. Lacking this skill puts people at a significant disadvantage, and literacy rates amongst the prison population are particularly notable. According to a recent report in *The Guardian*:

50% of prisoners in the UK are functionally illiterate. This means half of the 85,000 people currently incarcerated have a reading age of 11 or lower – with 20% falling well short of that mark. Many prisoners are completely illiterate.

(Moss, 2017)

Gary Wilson, a leading expert on boys' achievement, notes that less than half the homes in the UK have dinner tables around which families can gather, and this is having a negative impact in terms of communication skills (Wilson, 2013). He claims that boys in particular need the appropriate vocabulary not just for academic success but so that they can begin to 'unclench their tender hearts' (Wilson, 2018). In other words, they must be supported and equipped to express their emotions through conversation.

In *The Significance Delusion* (2016), Gillian Bridge explores the fact that young people today are unhappier, and feel lonelier, than ever before. Clearly, this sad phenomenon has many complex contributing factors, but the rise of social media and the 'selfie' culture seems to be fuelling a sense of introspection in young people, and egocentric behaviours that are far from benign.

Bridge reminds us that the language we use as educators, and that we encourage our pupils to use, is fundamentally important in helping young people develop a sense of their own significance and resilience.

The more people attend to and then make references to others, the healthier they are. Use of more third-person pronouns is linked to more adaptive coping which, in turn, results in better overall health.

(Bridge, 2016: 65)

In the classroom, this could mean we encourage pupils to use, '*he, she, they, his, hers* and *their*' and reference other people's ideas and achievement. Using a variety of pronouns along with '*we, us* and *our*' (not '*I, me* and *mine*') when reporting back from a collaborative learning experience helps pupils to appreciate the role and significance of individuals within a group dynamic.

On another practical level, scaffolding classroom dialogue using conjunctions such as 'in addition', 'furthermore', 'on the other hand', etc. also helps to develop this sense of connectivity. All of the vocabulary activities within this book can be easily adapted to emphasise the kind of beneficial language suggested by Bridge.

6. Collaborative learning

When successfully developed in the classroom, collaborative learning has the potential to extend and elevate pupils' learning past the superficial and into the deeper levels of understanding.

> *The impact of collaborative approaches on learning is consistently positive. Effective collaborative learning requires much more than just sitting pupils together and asking them to work in a group; structured approaches with well-designed tasks lead to the greatest learning gains. [...] Approaches which promote talk and interaction between learners tend to result in the best gains. [...] There is also indirect evidence that has shown that collaboration can increase the effectiveness of other approaches such as Mastery learning*

> *or Digital technology. Collaborative learning appears to work well for all ages if activities are suitably structured for learners' capabilities and positive evidence has been found across the curriculum.*

> **(Education Endowment Foundation, 2018)**

Most teachers would say that they incorporate group work in their classrooms. However, it is true to say that often pupils seem to be working in groups but not necessarily as groups. To capitalise on the merits of collaboration and make a significant impact on learning, teachers have to provide structure and support so that pupils have a varied set of opportunities to work together effectively. Through exposure to lots of challenging collaborative activities, pupils can start to appreciate that great minds do not necessarily think alike, and learn to value individual differences. In addition, they extend their appreciation of each other as learning resources to draw upon:

> *Learning is social. What children learn through social interaction with adults and peers forms the basis for more complex thinking and understanding. Over time, these skills, learning, and thinking processes become internalized and can be used independently.*

> **(Frey, Fisher and Everlove, 2009: 14)**

It is important to nurture the main components of successful collaboration so that pupils can understand that they are in a 'climate of allies', in which they feel supported to challenge and extend one another's thinking without making themselves vulnerable. Robin Banerjee's influential work on the social and emotional aspects of learning (SEAL) found that:

SEAL implementation and school ethos were directly associated with attainment results, as well as having an indirect connection with attainment via their link with positive behaviour. The connections between social and emotional ethos and better attainment, behaviour, and attendance remained significant after controlling for variations that are due to socio-economic status.

(Banerjee, 2010: 5)

⬤ Metacognition and self-regulated learning | Emotional engagement ▲ Retrieval and revision

Using strategies that link to this theme will allow you to provide a variety of collaborative experiences for your pupils. These will foster vital social communication skills whilst encouraging both individual accountability and positive interdependence.

Teachers are full of creativity and it is our hope that you will enjoy tweaking and personalising these techniques. Before we get to the fun bit, we just have to make a serious point. Some of the techniques we suggest involve fixing things to the ceiling or high up on the walls. Obviously we expect you to take all sensible and necessary precautions when doing this. Always work in line with your school's health and safety policy relating to heights and suspending objects overhead. We also don't want to get you into trouble, so always remember to check your school's policy on using hooks, tape and so on in the classroom before getting stuck in.

You will quickly notice that we have deliberately and unashamedly exploited the use of alliteration to make the key principles and strategies easily identifiable and memorable. We hope names such as 'Magpie Me' (see Chapter 4) will be easy to remember and use – and thus move from theory into classroom practice – and also facilitate discussion and reflection with colleagues. (Feel free to rename them in your implementation if the alliteration grates, though.)

We also encourage you to use this book to create your own annotated record. You could start by taking photos of your classroom as it looks currently and logging the techniques you try. We've deliberately included extra, blank bullet points at the end of each chapter for you to add your own creative ideas. Finally, we'd be really keen for you to share your experiences with us on social media using #DynamicallyDifferentClassrooms.

Chapter 1

BEYOND DISPLAYS:
FROM STATIC TO DYNAMIC

In this chapter

Whilst this book is about rethinking the use of the entire classroom space, and starting to extend the approach into the wider school environment, the obvious starting point for most teachers is to rethink their displays. We invite you to consider how your walls can become more than structural supports, by functioning as interactive agents for deeper learning, social interaction and individual growth. As outlined in the introduction, more than ever, teachers are recognising the value of metacognition and this chapter focuses on a highly visible and accessible way of placing this at the forefront of classroom practice.

Sound familiar?

Teachers invest a lot of time and energy producing attractive wall displays of which they can be proud. However, we would like to ask the question, 'If it is merely beautiful, why not just put up Laura Ashley wallpaper?' Having worked in hundreds of schools over the years, we have come across many well-intentioned policies and guidelines for displays. Indeed, we remember well the days of triple mounting and neatly aligned staples. Whilst many of these policies aim to create attractive and stimulating environments, they are often concerned primarily with aesthetics and with the outcomes of pupil and staff work. They also tend to assume that any information presented on the walls is automatically being noted, understood and retained by all pupils.

Perhaps this is hardly surprising when we consider some definitions of the word 'display':

❯ A collection of objects arranged for public viewing.

❯ A show or event staged for public exhibition or entertainment.

Even when used as a verb – 'to put something in a prominent place so that it may readily be seen' – the implied action is relatively finite. Once again the emphasis is on the product. As a result, walls are often used to house attractive but static displays of finished work. Whilst celebrating pupils' achievements is undoubtedly important, this approach does little to support them and move their learning forward.

So what needs to happen?

Repurposing

For all our well-intentioned policies, and the effort put into creating displays, it can be argued that this is not having a significant enough impact on learning. Pupils are not routinely engaging with what is on their walls. The novelty of even the most striking display soon fades to 'wallpaper' and does little to actively engage the pupils in thinking about the content, even if it is occasionally referred to by the teacher.

As we've discussed, over-complex, bright, cluttered displays are not beneficial to learning. However, by consciously making thinking processes and pupil progress highly visible – through well-structured, purposeful and dynamic displays – these spaces can pay dividends.

The nasen guide mentioned in the introduction made the following recommendations in relation to classroom displays and pupils with SEND:

Ensure your displays:

> *Are informative, interactive and relevant*

> *Are uncluttered so that information can be easily found*

> *Can be seen from every position in the classroom and used regularly by all pupils as a point of reference*

> *Show a good use of colour – avoid white background and black text*

> *Show keywords that are understood by all pupils*

> *Celebrate pupils' work and make them feel valued.*

(nasen, 2015: 7)

These guidelines contain well-thought-out, useful advice that would actually benefit all pupils, not just those with SEND. However, it would be very easy to glance at this list and overlook a keyword: *'interactive'*. This is the overriding element we want you to think about as you move 'beyond displays'.

The EEF Teaching and Learning Toolkit demonstrates that teaching metacognition can have a very positive effect on pupils' outcomes.[1] Pupils must be supported to engage with challenging concepts and articulate and own their learning. If used to stretch pupils and engage them in active responses, wall display space becomes a vibrant, high-profile, public area for developing and refining higher-order thinking skills.

Reweighting

Wall space is limited, and therefore valuable, so ultimately it needs to cover those things that pupils find most difficult to understand and remember. There is a value judgement to be made here: the display you have in mind, or have historically used, may be beautiful. It may be celebratory. It may make the pupils feel proud … and all these points are important and have their place. But, the Pareto principle (named after the economist Vilfredo Pareto and also known as the 80/20 principle) reminds us that, surprisingly often, around 20% of the inputs lead to around 80% of the outputs (Koch, 2017). In education, this broadly means

---

1 See https://educationendowmentfoundation.org.uk/evidence-summaries/teaching-learning-toolkit/meta-cognition-and-self-regulation/.

that a relatively small number of vital concepts may hold significant value in terms of academic achievement. The challenge is to work out which concepts are the most essential in each subject, and so should be prioritised or front-loaded. Impactful content, we believe, should have priority when it comes to display space.

Also, size matters. Big messages need big writing – sometimes *very* big! Currently, many displays are essentially invisible to pupils due to the size of the lettering and the positioning – often high up or at the back of the classroom. Ask yourself, what is in the immediate eyeline of your pupils and what is on the peripheries? Is this weighted correctly? Are you doing enough with the space around the board, as this tends to be the focus of attention in most classrooms?

Principles to underpin your practice

> Maximise pupil engagement first and foremost. The walls don't just support the learning, they are the learning.

> Check that the time invested in setting up displays actually pays dividends. Are pupils being actively challenged to think, respond, reflect and remember?

> Acknowledge that not all displays need to be polished and static, but can be interactive working resources to which pupils regularly contribute, or even generate and manage themselves.

> Ensure that learning comes off the wall and into the lesson before travelling back to the wall for later retrieval.

> Remember that even small changes to displays can have a dramatic effect.

Practical techniques

Re-energising existing displays

First, let's start with some easy techniques to tweak the type of display you've probably already got in your classroom. They typically require a small amount of preparation but immediately increase the potential for active engagement and responses from your pupils.

 Reframing. Rewrite success criteria as questions and display these prominently alongside the finished product. For example, for a display of artwork, you could ask, 'Where can you see examples of perspective?' This simple change immediately challenges the pupils to think and respond, leading to rich opportunities for discussion, clarification of misconceptions and peer and self-assessment.

If we are serious about facilitating the deep learning required in the national curriculum, we need to go even further. For example, after an appropriate period of familiarisation time, remove some of the prompt words from the display, perhaps

The Great Fire of London

The great fire of London happened between 2nd and 5th September 2015

Class 4 Artwork inspired by Van Gogh's Starry Night

The fire began in a bakery on Pudding Lane

The fire lasted ten minutes and burned down half a house

The fire engines came and put out the fire

The facts have been changed. Which are still true and which are false?

Many houses were made from wood and straw

False

True True

Class 4 are carrying out experiments. We have

replacing 'perspective' with 'p _____ '. Now pupils are being called upon to recall the word or concept. Finally, remove all the scaffolds, even the initial letter clue: what can pupils recall now?

Pick a Prompt. Distribute paper or cardboard thought and speech bubbles to encourage the use of speculative language. Ask pupils to use them to record their ideas, and position in appropriate places around the classroom to jump-start thinking and discussion. Some could have opening phrases like, 'Might …', 'Could it …', 'What if …', 'I think …', 'I wonder what …', 'This seems to suggest …', to which pupils can add their contribution. Laminating the bubbles has the extra benefit of encouraging pupils to take risks with their thought processes, as they can easily amend what they've written after discussion and rethinking. Plus laminated versions can be reused.

Label the Learning. This highlights the learning process as well as the end product. Invite pupils to review and respond to existing displays using symbols of their choice which they must:

> Annotate as fully as possible.

> Position where relevant on the wall.

> Be prepared to talk about.

You may find it helpful to provide some sentence stems to get them started – for example:

'This is a red herring because …'

'I/we want to challenge this ...'

'I/we would add ...'

'This links to ... because ...'

'I/we *now* think/know ... because ...'

'This is winning work because ...'

Using symbols can be very helpful in making each idea visual. For example, you could use the key:

fish = red herrings

question marks = challenges

arrows = linking ideas

addition signs = adding to an idea

rosettes = commending and annotating 'winning work'

Cut-out hands could also be used to offer a 'high five' or give a 'helping hand', with comments written along the fingers.

Tag It. Attach a pad of sticky notes and a pen to a display board for pupils to post comments, summaries, questions, etc., building in opportunities for pupils to do this until it becomes a routine expectation.

Revisit, Resurrect and Revive. As we've previously discussed, displaying exemplar work and making it effective and meaningful (and not just wallpaper) can be problematic. We have to ensure that it is being used dynamically. Re-examine existing exemplar displays by asking pupils questions like:

'What were you learning about here?'

'Are you still happy with this work?'

'Could you tell me more about ...?'

'Is there anything you would change?'

'How could you use this learning elsewhere?'

The emphasis here is on extending thinking, not merely remembering or revising. Establish the expectation that pupils will add extra ideas, reflective commentary, etc. to any 'finished' work that's on the walls. This approach also works well if pupils are asked to annotate photos of themselves engaged in a learning activity.

Extending the Thinking. Display questions alongside displays of the key learning. These could be phrased in a general way – for example, 'Can you explain/analyse/summarise this?' – or as a more subject-specific inquiry – for example, 'How can you use what you have learned about forces to explain why a boat floats in water?' You could extend the idea by asking differentiated questions, perhaps using a colour-coding system to indicate the level of challenge. The important aspect to stress here is that these are not merely rhetorical questions; they are there to be answered. Pupils need to *prove* that they have engaged with the questions, perhaps by adding their responses to an appropriate part of the display.

Dual Purpose. Use your permanent display boards for the most significant pieces of learning – for example, place value or exactly how to build a sentence. When appropriate, this can be temporarily overlaid with an attractive celebratory display of pupil work, mounted on large rolls of paper. The added benefit is that this can also be used to support memory challenges. What lies beneath? Can the pupils outline how the exemplar work demonstrates the learning that is now hidden?

Window of Opportunity. We all know how important it is to have natural light in the classroom and we're not suggesting sticking up large sheets of paper to block out the light or the view. However, the windows can become another really useful area for engaging learners. How about using the lower section to display questions, set challenges, etc.? If this is done so that it can be viewed from outside as well as inside the classroom, other learners and passers-by can be engaged and intrigued too.

Case study

Working window

We've seen a 'working window' put to good use in primary schools. One teacher had set up a double-sided place value chart, complete with bullet point reminders about multiplying and dividing, and every couple of days new questions would be posed. Evidence of engagement could easily be seen by the number of finger marks on the window!

In a different classroom, another teacher was also using this often neglected space. Her windows featured mathematical terms, exemplars and questions, which the children answered using window pens. A standard number line, displayed against the glass, featured laminated numbers annotated with the names of the pupils who had confidently mastered that times table. This celebrated and showcased achievement whilst encouraging pupils to focus on their next target.

Beyond the word wall

Displays of key vocabulary should be interactive and lively and should challenge the memory, rather than just providing a 'prop'. Tweaking, and thereby transforming, these displays generally requires little preparation but pays dividends by actively engaging pupils in thinking far more deeply and challenging their conceptual understanding.

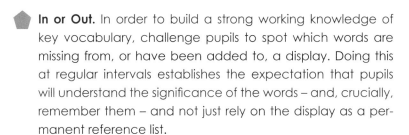

In or Out. In order to build a strong working knowledge of key vocabulary, challenge pupils to spot which words are missing from, or have been added to, a display. Doing this at regular intervals establishes the expectation that pupils will understand the significance of the words – and, crucially, remember them – and not just rely on the display as a permanent reference list.

Split Them Up. Separate key terms from their definitions and challenge pupils to rearrange the muddled pairs. This is an example of an easy 'simmering' activity that can quickly be targeted towards any pupils at any point in the lesson to keep previous knowledge fresh. You could also try organising this as a competition, with selected pupils being responsible for checking the matched pairs.

Prioritise. Ask pupils, 'Of the words displayed, which three are the most important to the topic of …?' Ask them to justify their choices. This oral rehearsal is a crucial precursor to any writing task.

Case study: Kirk Balk Secondary

Terminology team challenge

A group of Year 9 pupils had recently completed a full unit of work for the personal finance syllabus and were beginning to revise for their exam. Their teacher, Lynne, was keen to utilise the classroom itself in a more dynamic way, in order to lead to memorable and active revision. As the wall space was limited, she wanted to make use of a set of floor-to-ceiling cupboards with sliding doors for a revision activity.

The activity focused on using challenging subject-specific terminology which, perhaps unsurprisingly, pupils had found difficult to understand and assimilate into their knowledge. Lynne was keen to develop their confidence and familiarity with the key terms and, with this in mind, she had designed a set of questions and corresponding answers for the first part of the activity. These were cut up and placed into 'mystery envelopes', creating a sense of curiosity amongst the pupils.

The class was then split into two teams, on this occasion boys versus girls. The teams were set a timed challenge which involved competing to find the correct pairings as quickly as

⬤ Metacognition and self-regulated learning | Emotional engagement ▲ Retrieval and revision

possible. Next, pupils had to agree that they were all happy with each answer and confident that they would be able to explain them. Only then could they stick their answers up: each team working on opposite sides of the classroom, one using a wall and the other the cupboard doors. It was very interesting to observe the pupils' competitive nature starting to emerge as they watched the other team's progress literally take shape.

The next stage of the process involved pairs of pupils annotating the display by writing further details and linking connections on large yellow arrows for other pairs to critique and refine. It was interesting to see how the pupils readily used each other as learning resources to help clarify their understanding. They weren't prepared to just blindly accept someone else's opinion but instead stood their ground if they disagreed. There were some intense and productive discussions about the challenging terminology until the class arrived at an agreement. Lynne was freed to engage in some truly responsive teaching as she was able to circulate, ask challenging questions, address any misconceptions, support where appropriate and note possible areas for subsequent reteaching.

Taboo. Ask pupils to choose a few significant words from a key vocabulary display. Having written each one on a small postcard they then decide on four or five associated words that would help explain each term and list them underneath. Put the cards into a cardboard wallet or envelope and attach it in an appropriate position on a display board. At appropriate times pupils can work in pairs to try to describe the key term without saying any of the additional (Taboo) words on the card. Getting pupils to create the cards really challenges their understanding of the main ideas associated with the key vocabulary. They usually gain great satisfaction from trying to make the cards really difficult for other pupils.

Top Trumps. Top Trump cards score a series of related items according to a given set of criteria. For example, you could give key vocabulary items a score in terms of ease, complexity, usefulness, subject-relevance, etc. Asking pupils to justify and debate the scores they assign provides an additional challenge to their thinking. Similar to the Taboo cards, having your pupils collaborate to devise them really taps into higher-order thinking skills, as well as creating a game that can be used again and again.

Jeopardy. Hand each pair of pupils a card with a keyword written on it. You could target these towards particular pupils or use a random 'lucky dip' selection process. Pupils work in their pairs to come up with a question that would have the keyword as its answer. Again, use other pairs to check accuracy of responses.

Define and Defend. Provide sticky notes on which pupils can write the definition of a chosen word. Ask other pupils to critique the various definitions and jointly agree on a final version, which can be written up on the display. This can be another easy 'simmering' activity to make use of during lessons.

Odd One Out. Ask pupils to identify which keyword from a display is the odd one out and explain their reasoning. There won't necessarily be an obvious or correct answer but this will only enhance the thinking that has to go into the task.

Connect Four or More. Use your lists of key vocabulary to set up a giant, unlabelled display. Ask your pupils to identify and discuss patterns, connections and possible category headings. Large, colour-coded, laminated stars and arrows are especially helpful for adding key points and signposting the links. An added advantage is that they can be annotated with whiteboard markers to add further explanation. Or, as an alternative, imagine how this might work displayed on the ceiling with pupils being invited to use torches to trace the connections in a darkened classroom.

Inductive learning, including classification, is often underused but is a great way to engage pupils in a collaborative, analytical and speculative process that clarifies and deepens concept formation. Pupils will start to manipulate details into abstract categories and form generalisations and rules, but without being constrained by the notion of a predefined, single correct answer.

Metacognition and self-regulated learning | Emotional engagement ▲ Retrieval and revisic

Case study

Connections challenge

We saw a good example of the effectiveness of this technique in a Year 3 class. The teacher supplied a variety of adjectives and adverbs as a card-sort activity and trios of pupils were soon engrossed in grouping the different words. Within a few minutes, their discussions started to focus on the difference between adjectives and adverbs, before moving seamlessly into further analysis of the different types of adverbs and how they modified verbs. They then came up with subheadings to describe the different 'jobs' the adverbs did. It was also interesting to see the natural way in which those pupils who weren't sure about some of the words went over to talk with other groups rather than automatically asking the teacher. Their understanding was built on and challenged even more as the teacher uncovered a large-scale display of similar words and a supply of sticky notes and neon-coloured stars. Pupils were literally sitting on the edge of their seats as they anticipated their turn to go and connect four. The display was revisited over several lessons as pairs of pupils were invited to go and see if their learning was still live.

Using disruption

The next three ideas consist of 'disrupting' existing displays. Younger children really enjoy the idea that the 'elf on the shelf', class mascot or class pet has been up to mischief in the night and changed things around. One class we worked with took great pleasure in detecting the culprit responsible for the missing bits of their displays by finding 'half-chewed' remnants near the hamster cage. Some secondary school colleagues developed the idea that another teacher had played a prank on them and enlisted the help of their pupils to 'get their own back' by disrupting the culprit's classroom in a similar way.

Cover Up. Simply use sticky notes to cover parts of – or whole – words, phrases, sentences, images, etc. Challenge pupils to reproduce the hidden element. Working in pairs allows for discussion, clarification and highlighting misconceptions. Including the additional step of pairs having to obtain the agreement of the rest of the class before posting their ideas allows for further discussion, support and validation.

Mix Up. Remove something from or plant an extra something in an existing display – this could be a question, an unexpected stimulus or perhaps a red herring or odd one out. Challenge pupils to see if they can spot anything new.

Blanket Coverage. Place a sheet over a whole area overnight and organise a team competition to recreate what was there. This could be developed further in combination with the commonly used technique of pupils taking on the role of 'envoys' or 'magpies' to visit the other teams to give and take supplementary information.

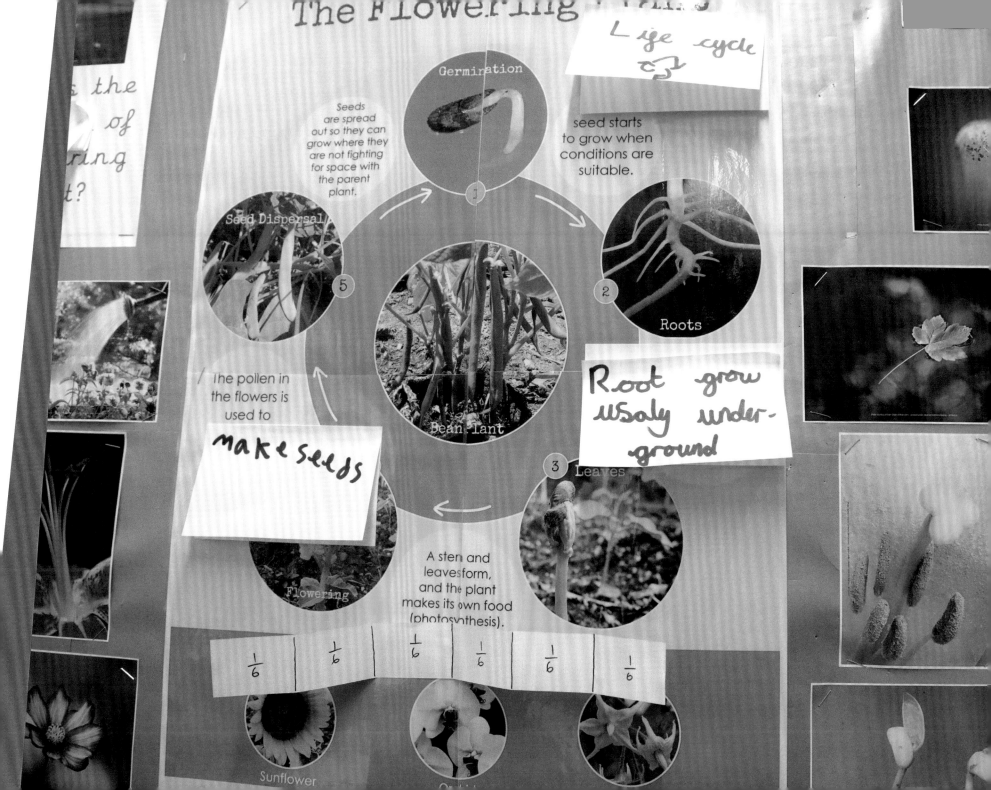

Case study: Darton Primary

The elf on the shelf

In this case, the school allowed us to take over a Year 3 classroom and tweak the existing displays in the fifteen minutes before the school day began. The emphasis was very much on low-preparation strategies that required little in the way of resources. The approaches included:

> Placing a toy elf on the shelf next to a prominent display along with the label, 'Can you spot what the elf on the shelf has changed overnight?'

> Covering up parts of a display of key scientific terminology using sticky notes – this included a selection of pictures, whole words and sentences and parts of them.

> Concealing a whole maths display about Roman numerals using a paper tablecloth labelled, 'What's behind here?'

> Covering up numbers in a counting in 50s display with a giant question mark.

> Adding different brightly coloured stars to a display of difficult spelling words (Year 3 and Year 4 level words containing one or two sets of double letters) along with the question, 'What might the coloured stars mean?'

> ❯ Concealing several of the 'W' prompts in the 'writing to inform' display – for example, where, who, when.

> ❯ Sticking large sheets of plain paper to the dead space below the main literacy display board to serve as an invitational writing surface (see The Bottom Line later in this chapter).

What happened?

From the moment the pupils entered the classroom, there was a genuine sense of intrigue and excitement with them quickly noticing both the elf on the shelf and the adaptations to the displays. Without any prompting at all, pupils immediately began to walk around the room and discuss what they thought might have changed, predicting what could be concealed.

We were keen to capitalise on this positive energy and pupils were allowed to self-select which of the challenges they wanted to tackle. This led to a very quick and easy grouping of pupils with the groups then immediately leaving their seats, approaching their chosen display area and getting to work.

Pupils at the science display began to look very closely at the still-visible cues and clues and discussed which words and images might be concealed. The sense of

challenge was evident as the children worked together to recall not just the general idea but the correct scientific terms. Collaborative working to check knowledge and understanding was prevalent as pupils asked each other a variety of questions, such as, 'What do you call that pointy thing again?' The stamen was the answer, in case you were interested.

Worth noting was the fact that in this situation the pupils were so engaged and self-directing that the teacher could be freed from delivering and able to move organically amongst the groups to observe, challenge and support where necessary. This change in role facilitates genuine reflection and response time within a very busy lesson, allowing the level of challenge to be easily adapted for those who need it. In the case of the group tackling the science display challenge, this took the form of an extension element: 'You need to work in pairs and agree on a definition with a different partner before adding your word to the wall.' For the group attempting to recreate what was hidden under the tablecloth, the introduction of a boys versus girls challenge led to intense and animated concentration from all the pupils.

The group focusing on the difficult spellings had to look very closely to begin to decode the connections between pink- and yellow-starred words. There was a great deal of exploratory talk and, once again, we insisted that pupils must agree their explanations before writing them up and adding to the display, leading to some very impressive turn-taking and active listening.

Another group tackled both the missing numbers and the missing features of writing to inform, also exhibiting high levels of collaboration and exploratory talk.

The final group was tasked with working together to draft some 'wow' sentences to add to the large sheets of paper below the literacy working wall. Pupils were told to peer assess each other's work against the features on the working wall before they could transcribe the sentences onto the paper. The novelty of using large marker pens led one pupil to exclaim, 'This feels really cool!'

When the groups had completed their chosen challenge we organised an easy extension and consolidation activity: each of the groups had to teach the rest of the class about what they'd learned. The pupils were given a few minutes to prepare and to decide how they were going to involve their 'audience'. Large foam Qs and Cs were used to signal various *questions* and *challenges*: the teachers could pose them to the class and the class to the teachers.

All of the groups rose to the occasion. The pupils moved effortlessly into 'teacher mode' and they all managed to engage the rest of the class through skilful questioning and setting little challenges. It was clear to see that the previous learning had been well and truly resurrected and revived and that the pupils had had fun in doing so. Pupil comments included:

> 'I was excited this morning because I didn't know what was going to happen and it was really fun.'

> 'I liked this morning because I didn't know what was going to happen because the cheeky elf had made my classroom really different.'

> 'I liked doing the spelling words because I wanted to see what the yellow and pink stars mean.'

> 'This morning was really good because we got to explore what had happened to the classroom overnight and we all got to work in different groups to do different things.'

> 'I liked it when we were the teachers and got to teach everybody and ask them questions.'

Thinking about new displays

Creating irresistible hooks

Draw Them In. Consider using a massive, magnified version of an intriguing image plastered across a wall but with no explanation or instructions. Leave it there so pupils begin to preprocess and speculate. Images by illustrators such as Shaun Tan, Anthony Browne or Roberto Innocenti would work wonderfully due to their intriguing nature.

Powerful Projection. Create a truly immersive atmosphere by dimming the lights and projecting an image onto the ceiling. Imagine the impact and memorability of having pupils lie on the floor and look up at a projection of an image or video – for example, of the solar system, a volcanic eruption, a natural disaster, a painting, etc. – whilst considering some key questions. You could develop this further by incorporating appropriate audio commentary or questions asked by your previous pupils.

The Mouth of Truth. Borrowing from the Bocca della Veritá, or Mouth of Truth, which is a large Roman stone disc carved into the shape of a humanoid face, with hollow holes for eyes. Its gaping mouth is said to bite the hand of anyone who lies. Use a decorated cardboard box to recreate a similar model. Fill the mouth with pieces of paper containing written statements and challenge pupils to pull these out one at a time and prove whether or not they are true. The requirement for pupils to 'prove' their thinking with evidence generates high-quality investigative learning. In addition, this

approach can be used for any topic and works really well as a revision activity if the statements are related to prior learning.

An alternative adaptation could be to play up the idea of concealment and secrecy. Your Mouth of Truth could be used to house a whole range of mysterious prompts – such as, intriguing objects, text snippets, challenges, etc. At unexpected moments, pupils could be chosen to dip their hands into the void and pull something out. This would work brilliantly for re-energising lessons.

Variations could include:

> Colour-coded challenges – for example, red ones relating to prior learning, blue for current learning. This approach functions very effectively as a way of checking that learning is still live.

> Mysterious objects to be unwrapped as a group, Pass the Parcel style. Have pupils organise this activity.

> A coded message that, when solved, supplies a key word or phrase. Increase the intrigue by including the name of someone else in the school – such as the head teacher – to whom the pupil must go in order to 'take delivery' of their main challenge or activity. We have found that pupils respond well to the involvement

of other adults in their learning, and often add a VIP element to enhance an activity. There is more on this in Chapter 2.

Gift Bags. Make use of potentially dead space on the lower part of a wall. Put up sticky hooks (the kind you can take down and reuse) and suspend brightly coloured gift bags from them. The bags look very attractive and can be used to intrigue the pupils, especially if they are labelled with tantalising invitations, such as 'Mystery challenges: dip in when ready' or 'Help yourself'. The gift bags are a very effective way to support pupils to work independently and could contain a whole variety of stimuli. For example:

> Key vocabulary and/or a range of punctuation marks alongside an appropriate challenge.

> Different classes of words in different bags – for example, nouns, verbs, adverbs, connectives, etc. An example task could be, 'Take a word from each bag and see if you can use them to make a good sentence.'

> Pictures to promote discussion or stimulate writing.

> A variety of exam questions for pupils to answer.

> Different artefacts to discuss and classify.

> Statements to be sorted into true and false piles.

> Anything else you can think of?

Cabinet of Curiosities. Use an actual cabinet or cupboard to house curiosities – for example, artefacts, intriguing images, etc. This works effectively in its own right, but combining it with 'treasures' generated by your pupils, both past and present, makes it even more powerful. The cabinet becomes a repository of pupils' 'prove it' tasks, proud moments, photos, etc. and serves to inspire other learners, as a legacy of the learning. The contents of your cabinet have the potential to be used as different types of thought-provoking stimuli for resurrecting and reviving prior learning. For more about cabinets of curiosity, we'd recommend *The Little Book of Awe and Wonder* by Matthew McFall (2013).

Evolving, learner-generated displays

KWLP grids. You are probably already familiar with the idea of kick-starting new topics by allocating a blank display area as a KWL grid (already *know*, *want* to find out about, have *learned* about). The K column is particularly important as it informs teachers what pupils' existing knowledge base is, thereby informing future planning. Over subsequent lessons, pupils add to the display using the knowledge they have gained. The emphasis should be on pupils routinely making active contributions during lesson time.

In order to facilitate even deeper learning, try adding an extra column: P (the *prove it* place), where pupils are required to demonstrate their learning in a format of their own choosing at a later date. Once a concept is fully understood, pupils can be genuinely creative in how they present it. This is an ideal place to capture evidence of the *transposition* of

learning – for example, across the curriculum and beyond the school. Imagine a pupil photographing themselves teaching this topic to someone at home, and displaying this with a commentary focusing on how they prepared and how they felt. This is the kind of innovative and far-reaching learning you get in a dynamically different classroom.

Prod and Prickle. Experiment with making displays deliberately provocative – for example, with an incorrect statement, quote, equation, etc. that pupils have to respond to or correct using evidence. This could take the form of sticky notes, group responses or 'graffiti' directly on the display.

Park It Board. Have a designated place where pupils can 'park' any idea that they feel needs to be flagged, either because it is particularly significant, challenging or contentious, or needs further explanation. As pupils grow in independence this can be done without teacher direction.

Teacher No-Go Domain. Set up designated pupil-managed display boards which pupils can use to:

> Set challenges for their classmates.

> Interpret the learning in their own way, ideally during the lesson. For example, using the structure 'This makes me think of/makes me feel/reminds me of …'

> Display their WOMBOLLs (what one of my best ones looks like).

⬤ Metacognition and self-regulated learning ｜ Emotional engagement ▲ Retrieval and revision

Case study: The Dearne ALC[2]

'Beat my best' board

This English lesson took place in a shared classroom. Sometimes this may mean that wall space is disputed territory or in short supply. However, the teachers had got around this difficulty by making use of portable boards on wheels that could travel easily as needed. Joanne used a portable board to create a 'Beat My Best' display, showing what pupils had scored in practice exam questions over a period of time. Most teachers store this information routinely in their marks books or similar. Indeed, many schools now have flightpath software that might even allow pupils to log in to update and review their progress. So, we could question why we'd bother making a large-scale version for display. This display was certainly not an attractive or dynamic one: however, creating a glossy, finished product wasn't Joanne's intention. This was an invitational tool which was used to engage pupils with physically tracking and celebrating their incremental progress over time. Not only were pupils adding their scores to the board but, crucially, they were also taking formative feedback from the summative data in the form of areas to target for improvement.

As pupils updated the board with their latest scores, they automatically began to discuss and celebrate their progress. Furthermore, they were beginning to 'skill swap' independently and to share their expertise in the areas where they had scored well. They were obviously appreciating the value of using each other as a learning resource. Clearly, this was all taking place within a classroom ethos of allies, not judges, which had been actively fostered by the teacher over time. The only competition was with themselves, not with each other.

Joanne also included a fun technique that appealed to the pupils' adolescent sense of humour. She invited them to select a colourful emoji sticker to signal where they had responded to feedback and consistently achieved. This was not tokenism or pandering to their interests, but a tongue-in-cheek approach that really aided memorability. There was a lot of good-natured banter as the pupils made their selection and compared their choices.

---

2 Now called Astrea Academy Dearne.

Marketplace. Split the class in half and then divide one half into subgroups of three. Allocate the trios of pupils an area of the classroom in which they have to speedily put together a temporary display of key information relating to different aspects of a unit of work. Follow this up by having them 'make their pitch' or 'sell their wares' to the rest of the class, who circulate and visit the different stalls in this learning marketplace. Get pupils to critique the temporary displays and mini-presentations. Repeat this process at a later point, reversing the roles. Another possibility could be to use this approach to complete a task or question. This time, divide the whole class into teams to compete against the clock to generate the most ideas and solutions and get these on the board first.

Another Brick in the Wall. Invite pupils to build up displays over a series of lessons. Begin with a completely blank wall and invite pupils to offer up key learning points over time, literally adding information brick by brick. This can then be used dynamically – for example, for concept mapping, inductive learning activities and odd-one-out challenges. A seasonal alternative could be to use Christmas tree shapes and ask pupils to annotate each branch with keywords, ideas, pictures, etc. Then use the trees to build up a forest of the term's learning.

The Bottom Line. Attach wallpaper or backing paper to the bottom half of a wall, which is within the eyeline of younger children and provides easy access. This creates an ideal and very inviting space which can be used for a multitude of activities, from early mark making in reception through to more sophisticated usage for older learners. You can do this by adding long lengths from these rolls of paper and encouraging pupils to use this as a space in which to respond creatively and independently to the topic – for example, by drafting questions, adding vocabulary, illustrating, etc.

Analogy Alley. This involves pupils creating analogies as a way of understanding new or complex concepts. This time, in preparation for a display, pupils decide what analogy or image would be useful to symbolise a particular aspect of the current learning, offering an appropriate title – for example, 'Bullying is like …', 'Equations are like …', 'Macbeth is like …' Keep going back to these and challenging pupils to explain the analogy. Probing is key in checking for and preventing incomplete understanding and deciding where and how to reteach specific aspects. This technique can be made more challenging by taking the titles away and asking pupils to recall what the analogy represents.

Gamification

Board Games Repurposed. Games are another great way to engage pupils, especially when coupled with the randomness factor generated by something like dice-throwing. By allocating wall space and displaying large versions of your selected boards you are generating several extra benefits: you are prioritising and showcasing the importance of the identified focus; you are making the interaction much more dynamic, energised and memorable by having pupils move and stand whilst playing the game; and you are sparking the interest of the class. Creating a board that requires pairs of pupils to collaborate to answer increasingly difficult questions, or practise specific skills around high-priority areas of the curriculum, allows for a depth of discussion that might not usually be so forthcoming. Incorporating aspects which move the players backward (as in snakes and ladders) can be a sneaky way to increase practice time. Variations could include replacing the usual squares on the board with triangles or hexagons so that multiple, possibly differentiated, routes can be taken by the pupils. You could also keep A4 or A3 printed versions at the side in clearly labelled plastic wallets, ready for pupils to select at strategic times.

Roll the Dice. (Also known as Learning Grids.) Basically, this uses 6 x 6 grids which can have a variety of images, words and phrases or instructions in each of the cells. The grid structure allows for different levels of challenge and creativity. Pupils work in pairs and roll dice to determine which cell they will start to think about. The randomness of dice-throwing, with the element of both fairness and anticipation, is a great motivator. This combination makes for a really effective hook for pupils of all abilities.

We know lots of teachers who have developed a whole range of really effective Learning Grids: from examples used to develop storytelling with Year 1 to ones for GCSE organic chemistry revision that kept the group engaged and working at a faster rate than the teacher had thought possible. *Engaging Learners* by Andy Griffith and Mark Burns (2012) gives lots of other great examples.

Case study: Hoyland Common Primary

Learning leaping off the walls

Pupils had been studying rivers and had worked with their teacher, Rosie, to create a visually striking display that was operating on several sophisticated levels. It contained:

› An image showing both pupils' prior knowledge of the topic and questions identifying what they wanted to find out next in their learning. This was called a thought shower to link in with their topic.

› Sticky notes containing pupils' initial ideas which could be refined and improved throughout the learning process.

› Extra sticky notes and a pen, attached to the wall, inviting pupils to make further contributions as their learning evolved.

› A particularly intriguing and challenging 'big question' for pupils to ponder and preprocess: 'If water is flowing down a river to the sea, why doesn't the river run empty?'

Pupils were automatically interacting with this display on a frequent basis, posting their own questions and suggested answers and using it as a repository for all their learning and to feed their next steps. It is hard to describe just how much genuine enthusiasm the pupils were showing.

Whilst working on their history project about the Second World War, Rosie had once again set out to exploit the potential of classroom display areas as interactive learning tools with which her class readily engaged. Pupils had devised questions and written these on luggage tags (like the ones worn by children during the evacuations of Operation Pied Piper). They then attached them to the display for other children to answer in red. Any further feedback on the answers was offered in a different colour. These colour distinctions made it easier for pupils and the teacher to focus on different parts for critique and to suggest additions or changes. In another area of the classroom, ration books were available with the expectation that pupils would keep a record of their understanding by writing down the facts they'd learned and the questions they still had.

Another major way in which Rosie had really embraced this interactive potential was by posting QR codes that linked to videos that the pupils had made following their 'Escape to the Country', a Second World War evacuee experience day at the nearby Cannon Hall Farm. The children then scanned the codes and used the links to the videos to support their research as they continued working on their project. The children were also asked to use apps like Explain Everything to talk about a series of photographs relating to the Second World War and explain what they had learned and enjoyed.

The grids work really well in A4 format but, as in the previous board games example, allocating a large display space for a super-sized grid makes the activity even more dynamic as pupils can go up and throw over-sized dice to allocate their tasks. Having pairs of pupils write their names on the square they are attempting is a useful technique, as pupils with related tasks can identify where they might seek collaborative allies. Try incorporating some challenges in the grid – that can be colour-coded to denote the level of difficulty (for example, a red hot or purple power challenge) – accompanied by a large symbol that the pupils can place on their desks to signify that they are attempting something demanding. This can signal the need for uninterrupted concentration, support, a debriefing plenary, etc.

Encouraging pupils to become learning resources for one another

Calendar Challenge. You could revamp an Advent calendar by creating a large-scale one with challenges, questions, photos or similar behind each window. Create a significant daily moment by focusing the whole class' attention on the calendar and randomly selecting a pupil to open the window and take on the challenge. The pupil could choose to work on the activity on their own or enlist help from volunteers. Names or photos could then be stuck in the open window as an 'Ask me about my Calendar Challenge' prompt. Making this display space highly visual creates a sense of anticipation and also prompts visitors to the classroom to discuss the learning challenges.

Or how about working with pupils to create an Advent calendar with key ideas, words and images about a topic they've just learned for next year's class to open and use the following December? This could use a countdown approach with the more straightforward aspects of the learning being revealed first, leading up to one big idea, question, class challenge, etc.

Whispering Wall. Have an accessible space where pupils can listen to or record helpful tips. Dry-wipe, recordable speech bubbles can be used for this (these are readily available from a range of online suppliers). They can also be used by pupils to critique, question and add to other display areas. The whole class can listen to the recordings and then discuss what they've heard.

Really Useful Stuff Board. Pupils discuss, decide upon and depict important things to remember about specific aspects of units of work and display them outside their classroom for other pupils to see. You might find it useful to suggest sentence stems – for example, 'The most important thing to remember about … is …' Add an extra plastic wallet to the display, filled with blank cards so that passers-by can take them and add their ideas as well. An alternative could be for pupils to create audio versions as podcasts. These learner-generated prompts are useful for clarifying understanding for revision purposes but could also be saved and used with a new group or class as a precursor to the start of a topic.

Critique Circuit. The emphasis here is on an area of current learning. Following the appropriate modelling of expectations and time spent practising, pupils could be invited to go on a Critique Circuit – or Progress Parade, if you prefer – to critique each other's work and offer SWAN feedback (about *strengths*, *weaknesses* and *next steps*). The idea of pupils commenting on weaknesses in others' work may ring alarm bells with some teachers; however, if time has been spent developing a genuine climate of 'allies not judges', then constructive feedback will be appreciated as playing a vital role in everyone's progress. Pupils could use sticky notes, speech or thought bubble cards to do this. Or you could create a supply of cut-out swans for them to write the feedback on, thus making the expectations even more overt and memorable. In addition, you could use cut-out magpies for the pupils to indicate the ideas they would steal.

Developing more independence

Get Set, Go. Get pupils used to working without an explanatory introduction. Try setting up systems where the instructions and resources for the session's activities and different pupil roles are obtained from a specific place – for example, centrally on the tables, in an agreed position on a wall, etc. This could be done in a very engaging way by concealing the instructions or objectives around the classroom – perhaps in sealed envelopes hidden as cryptically as you desire for your class – and treating it as an exploration or treasure hunt. If your school has the infrastructure in place, these could be sent directly to pupils via email, text message, etc., which has the added potential of engaging them before they even arrive at school.

 Moving On. Pupils choose the appropriate media to highlight or record a significant point in their learning and explain how they moved on from this – using a personalised learning log, for example. This serves primarily as an opportunity for true self-reflection and analysis but could easily be developed as advice for other pupils. The media could be visual, for placing in a designated area, or a short video which could become part of a blog or vlog.

The focus could be on:

> My motivating mistake.

> My muddiest moment.

> My light bulb moment.

> My key learning point.

> My challenging bit.

> My eureka moment (how I became unstuck).

> My stumbling block.

You could make this last idea more physical by using nets which pupils could write on and then construct into cubes – their literal stumbling blocks (an idea we explore further in Chapter 3). Others can roll these when completed and discuss how to address the different sides of the issue.

Learning Journeys. How about plotting the learning for a particular unit of work as a large-scale journey plan or map on the wall? Pupils can create their own learning avatar and decide where they are and what their next steps should be. The avatar could be made simply by using a cut-out card shape or be a more elaborate design made using any suitable software. This can then be positioned to show a pupil's movement along the physical learning journey and updated as more skills are acquired. This links well to the idea of gaining and repeatedly applying new learning powers or skills. Pupils could literally fill up their avatars by annotating them with new skills as they demonstrate them.

Or, instead of skills, they could be annotated with examples of how the pupil has actively done something that exemplifies the spiritual, moral, social and cultural development (SMSC) curriculum. Or, how about pupils personalising their avatar by adding their targets, an inspirational quote, etc.? An extra motivating element could be to introduce learning labels. Each time pupils have successfully demonstrated desired skills or behaviours – such as working with other people effectively, expanding their ideas, developing their resilience, etc. – this can be recorded on a sticky note and placed onto their avatar. A friendly competition could be encouraged to see who can collect the most.

Interesting discussions can be had about what imagery could be used to signify challenges, easy bits, time out to rethink, chances to retry, barriers, key points, etc. Some of our favourite examples that teachers and their classes have developed include:

> A racing track with pit stops, roundabouts, uphill and downhill climbs, milestone markers and a chequered flag, which signalled that learners had to prove it by teaching someone else.

> A walk through the countryside complete with clear paths, overgrown bits, fences, large holes, rivers and a hill, providing a view from the top.

> A flight path with pre-flight checks, take-off, dealing with turbulence, safe landing and transit to the next stage of the journey.

Remember When. (Also known as Déjà Vu.) Create a photo gallery showing pupils engaged in a particularly significant or challenging aspect of their learning. These could be examples of individual or collaborative learning. Ideally, have a tablet – or any other device with a camera – on-hand at all times and foster the expectation that pupils will be photographers whenever they see, or are involved in, something worth capturing.

Display each photo in a frame within a frame, on which pupils can annotate their learning. You could achieve this effect using two pieces of different coloured paper. The inner frame can be used for more straightforward comments, recorded at a time close to the point of learning, responding to prompts like:

> What were you learning?

> What were you doing?

❯ How did you feel?

❯ Anything else you can think of?

Annotate the outer frame at a later date, increasing the level of challenge and checking for long-term retention, by posing questions such as:

❯ What do you remember?

❯ What were the success criteria?

❯ What key vocabulary can you use now?

❯ What went well?

❯ Was anything difficult?

❯ What helped you?

❯ What could you have improved?

❯ Where else might you use the things you learned?

❯ Anything else you can think of?

Of course, this whole technique could be made more 'powerfully playful' by challenging pupils to tackle more of the bullet point prompts each time they are set this kind of photographic memory challenge. Alternatively, you could number the prompts and have pupils roll a die to determine the question they answer. This could be made even more challenging by covering up all of the photos, revealing them at strategic times in order to resurrect and revive the learning.

An added benefit of this approach is that it helps busy teachers to easily remember a wide range of pedagogies that they can draw on in their teaching. Even better, teachers can use these prompts to co-construct the learning with their pupils – for example, by asking, 'If we are learning …, how could we do that best?' 'What activities from the photo gallery have worked well in the past?'

Nurturing the powers of aspiration and iteration

Famous Failures. We have often seen posters featuring inspiring quotes by famous people displayed in classrooms. However, if we really feel these examples are useful in helping our pupils to develop resilience and growth mindsets then we need to use real-life stories of endeavour and perseverance in the most dynamic way possible. So use examples of people who pupils know of and who have become very successful because of their repeated attempts to achieve in their field.

The billionaire James Dyson is a good example. Very few people know that it took 5,127 prototypes before the first Dyson vacuum cleaner was considered ready for market (see Loftus, 2011): now there's a man who believes in the power of yet (see Dweck, 2014).

Another good example would be the famous quote delivered by basketball superstar Michael Jordan in a Nike commercial, 'I've missed more than 9,000 shots in my career. I've lost almost 300 games. 26 times, I've been trusted to take the game-winning shot and missed. I've failed over and over and over again in my life. And that is why I succeed.'[3] These examples are definitely very inspiring but rather than merely displaying them and creating another piece of wallpaper, try separating the people from the statistics within a large-scale display and challenge pupils to match the person to the number of mistakes. Or conceal the number of failures and invite the pupils to guess the figure. This one is well worth trying if only to hear the audible gasps at some of the numbers. This focus on mistake-making reinforces the idea of true progress happening over time and the importance of feedback to progress. Then ask pupils to put up statistics about their own personal experience of failure alongside the display – again, in a culture of allies not judges this shouldn't prove too daunting.

Process or Product? If you agree that the examples of famous failures are important, we would challenge you to look honestly at the type of pupil work that currently makes it onto your display boards. Is it often polished and best work – the equivalent of Dyson's finished vacuum cleaner? This does pupils a disservice by implying that such work somehow materialised out of nowhere. Far better to ensure that displays routinely include examples of work in process alongside end products. Ideally, such displays would also include large-scale annotations with comments from the pupils showing exactly how they moved from one stage or draft to the next. Just as we aim for 'process praise' in the classroom

– where we celebrate the effort that went into the creation above the final outcome – this technique echoes that ethos in the physical environment.

Another really good resource is the somewhat ubiquitous video about Austin's butterfly (EL Education, 2012). Sharing this video of Ron Berger involving pupils in a 'gallery critique' of Austin's work is a quick and powerful way to begin to train your class to do the same for each other. Why not try printing off copies of the six drafts he drew of the butterfly and displaying them side by side along with some of the Berger's key feedback mantras – for example, 'Be easy on the people, tough on the ideas' (Berger, Woodfin and Vilen, 2016: 194). Then involve your pupils in displaying examples of their own iterative processes in a similar layout.

WAGOLL Versus WASOLL. Use a prominent display space to actively engage pupils in the reflective analysis of success criteria, developing this further into the realms of co-construction. Having a large-scale example of a WAGOLL (what a good one looks like) and a WASOLL (what a substandard one looks like – also known as a WABOLL, or what a bad one looks like) within the enabling classroom provides pupils with an instant point of comparison for their own work. 'How does mine look at the moment?' 'What specific things do I need to do to make it more like a WAGOLL?' Developing the ability to analyse specific features of good and substandard work is crucial if we want pupils who

---

3 https://www.youtube.com/watch?v=45mMioJ5szc.

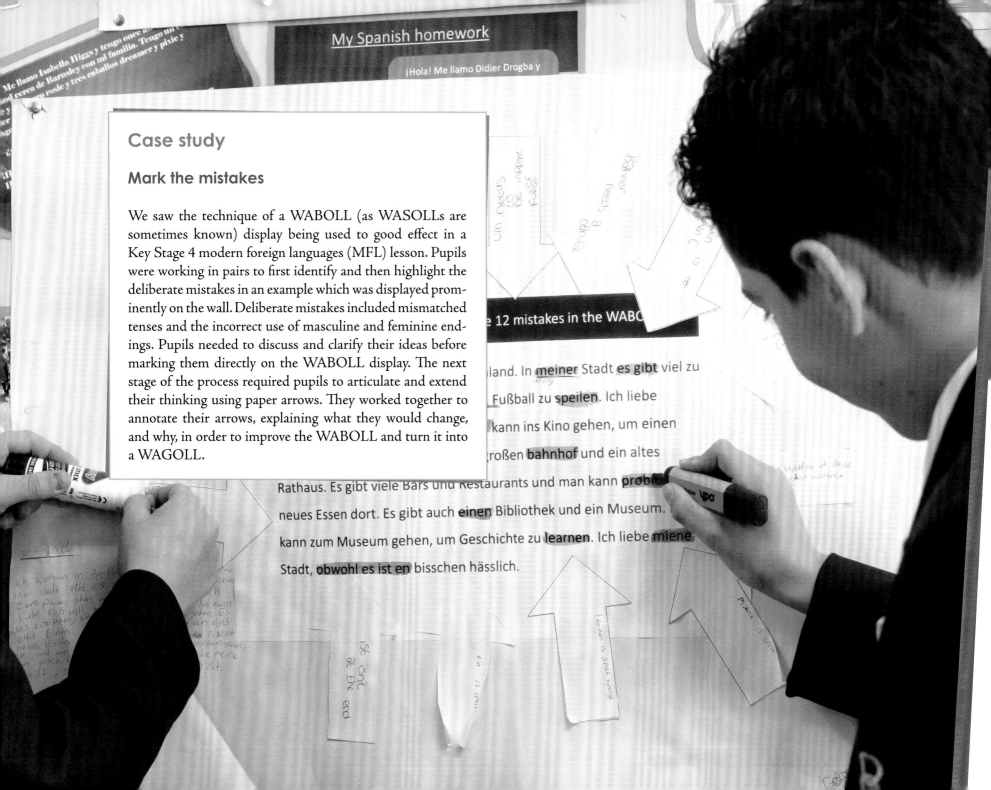

Case study

Mark the mistakes

We saw the technique of a WABOLL (as WASOLLs are sometimes known) display being used to good effect in a Key Stage 4 modern foreign languages (MFL) lesson. Pupils were working in pairs to first identify and then highlight the deliberate mistakes in an example which was displayed prominently on the wall. Deliberate mistakes included mismatched tenses and the incorrect use of masculine and feminine endings. Pupils needed to discuss and clarify their ideas before marking them directly on the WABOLL display. The next stage of the process required pupils to articulate and extend their thinking using paper arrows. They worked together to annotate their arrows, explaining what they would change, and why, in order to improve the WABOLL and turn it into a WAGOLL.

are capable of critiquing their own efforts and providing meaningful feedback to one another. This is at the heart of what Dylan Wiliam (2006: 8) describes as pupils becoming 'instructional resources for each other' and 'owners of their own learning'.

Encourage pupils to design their own examples to be displayed under the heading 'WAGOLL or WASOLL?' Other pupils then identify whether the example is good or not before annotating and improving it. This would ensure that one display continues to evolve and change regularly, and remains in active use, but without further teacher input.

On This Day. This technique lends itself better to primary pupils, as you can see more pronounced developmental differences in their work. On the same day, invite every pupil in the school to complete the same task – for example, painting a bird, flower or still-life. This would work equally well with a writing or reading response task. Next, display the work (or a rotating selection of examples) in a prominent whole-school space, such as the dining hall. Label with an appropriate, inspirational title. Here we are reminding all pupils that they are on a journey of progression. We are harnessing the celebration of current learning with the motivational elements of aspiration and inspiration for future learning and progress, all in the same display.

Rolling Forward. At the end of each year, make large copies of significant pieces of pupils' work ('our best so far …'). Pass these on to their next class or subject teacher, who can mount them on one end of a roll of paper – wallpaper or

backing paper would work well here. The remaining space can initially include examples of new learning and, later, reworked versions. This is an effective way to demonstrate the progression of learning. Leave space for 'our very best work', and for annotations to justify why it is.

Front-loading

Big Question. If there is an overall big question in the topic that pupils will be expected to be able to answer, or an end-of-unit assessment, consider bringing this forward, displaying it prominently and keeping it in the pupils' eyeline, perhaps floating in the middle of a display board with plenty of space around it for them to add contributions. This technique allows pupils to begin the crucial job of preprocessing by discussing and analysing what they will need in order to successfully attempt it. How are they going to research and acquire the requisite knowledge and skills? What help and support will they need? What form will their answer take – for example, must it be written? Or could the pupils use other media? If we are truly aiming for durable learning, rather than short-term performance, then surely we will want our pupils to have opportunities to attempt, reflect, revise and improve through several iterations rather than be assessed on a high-stakes, one-off basis.

Big Picture. Consider sharing the overall plan for a future unit of work with pupils, either on a large sheet of paper (A3 minimum) or electronically, but keep this visible and accessible within the lesson. Encourage suggestions about how the learning might take place, and ask pupils to add their

Case study: Hoyland Common Primary

Compete to the beat

The teacher, Rosie, had set up a 'WAGOLL or WASOLL?' board which she used in a particularly creative way with her Year 3 class. She displayed the exemplar text on the whiteboard whilst also pointing out a version on the wall. Pupils were given one minute to silently read the on-screen version and decide whether they thought it was a WAGOLL or a WASOLL. Next, Rosie played a vibrant piece of music, lasting two minutes. Whilst this was playing, pupils took it in turns to reach for a marker pen and edit the version on the wall to improve it in some way. They worked silently, without any teacher intervention, to the accompaniment of the music, and it was magical to watch the relay-like transitions as pupils quickly and enthusiastically passed the pen to the next volunteer in order to capture all their contributions on the wall.

Rosie noted that it was better to have these ideas captured on the wall as this had a longer-lasting impact than the interactive whiteboard screen, as it could be kept on display for pupils to refer to in their subsequent learning. It was clear that the pupils really enjoyed this activity too, commenting:

> 'It feels physically good to do this.'

> 'It's fun and challenging!'

ideas as annotations. Use this as an opportunity to secure their investment – for example, you could deliberately play to popular interests in gaming and challenge them to include ideas about how games could be used to support the intended learning. As a class, decide on the most appropriate aspects to adjust. A favourite memory from many years ago is when, having shared a humanities unit plan with a Year 8 class, a group of pupils not only came up with some really interesting ideas but put the whole explanation to music and presented it in a year group assembly. Needless to say, the ideas were incorporated and the pupils, and teachers, were completely engaged.

Big Flip. Many schools are using the idea of the 'flipped classroom' as a specific kind of enabler. This is a type of blended learning approach which 'flips' the traditional learning environment by delivering content outside of the classroom, often online. Pupils know what topic is coming up – for example, the Great Fire of London, the circulatory system, river environments, etc. – and are expected to preprocess and prepare, with lesson time then used to explore what they have researched. Tie this more explicitly to your classroom environment by setting aside a prominent display board on which pupils are expected and empowered to post their findings – in a form of their own choosing. Imagine the power of the first lesson of a new topic in which pupils can lead the learning using their display as the springboard.

And What Else?

>

>

>

>

>

>

>

>

>

>

We're ready to launch our learning!
But...
we'll be ready for 'Re-entry' later!

Chapter 2

NOTHING WASTED: STORING LEARNING TO RESURRECT AND REVIVE LATER

In this chapter

We explore how your whole classroom, and especially your ceiling, can take revision to a whole new level – quite literally. Leaving aside the obvious caveats about access and health and safety for the moment, it is possible to put ceilings to better use by repurposing them to function almost as 'cloud storage' for previous learning.

We invite you to capture the fleeting aspects of learning in order that they can have long-lasting impact, significance and relevance for your pupils. So much of what happens in classrooms is spontaneous and in the moment, and is often all the more magical for that. However, the current education system, driven by a prevalent test and exam culture, means that today's teachers are under increasing pressure to be 'accountable' and to demonstrate that pupils are making progress. Add to this the tension between performance and true, long-term learning (as explored in the introduction) and we seem to have a clear mandate for transforming the ephemeral into something more tangible and lasting.

Adopting the approach outlined in this chapter means that no inch of the classroom is underused and no evidence of learning is thrown away (even if it is a crumpled paper snowball, as we'll go on to see in Hidden in Plain Sight). Instead, save everything as a legacy of the learning and keep resurrecting and reviving it as part of the revision process. Ensure that this is done in a variety of ways. As we explored in the introduction, Bjork's 'desirable difficulties' remind us of the importance of varying the conditions

of practice. Exploit unpredictability of timing, resources and technique to maximise pupils' engagement and increase memorability even further.

Sound familiar?

Ceilings account for approximately one-sixth of the available surface space in any classroom, but this space is often used sparingly – if at all. Although we frequently see very attractive mobiles and washing lines dangling from ceilings, especially in early years and primary settings, perhaps we should apply the same caveat that we did with walls: beware that which is merely beautiful. The adornments on our ceilings can and ought to function in the same way as interactive wall displays. They should be visibly accessible and used to solicit an *ongoing* response from our learners.

So what needs to happen?

Put distance between the learner and the learning

Once again, we return to the work of Professor Robert Bjork and his important distinction between temporary performance and true long-term learning. Whilst we all know that this is important, it can be easy to lose sight of it in the busy day-to-day life of the classroom. The problem is further compounded by an overfull curriculum which often leads to a 'coverage' mentality. The ideas in this chapter provide a range of exciting and unusual strategies to keep the learning live by allowing pupils to interact with information in a variety of different ways over a period of time.

> *Interleaving benefits not only memory for what is studied, but also leads to benefits in the transfer of learned skills (e.g. Carson and Wiegand, 1979). The theory is that interleaving requires learners to constantly 'reload' motor programs (in the case of motor skills) or retrieve strategies/information (in the case of cognitive skills) and allows learners to extract more general rules that aid transfer.[1]*

In addition, Bjork's 'New Theory of Disuse' argues for the need to reduce the accessibility of information in order to generate additional learning of that information.[2] The techniques in this chapter put physical distance between the pupils and their prior learning – for instance, by hanging it from the ceiling or concealing it in sealed scrolls. By their very nature, they also introduce distance in terms of time as pupils will not be interacting with this information on a daily or even weekly basis. Rather, it will

be there safely in storage, or hanging above their heads, waiting for the appropriate time to be reintroduced and revived collaboratively.

Many of the approaches invite pupils not only to revisit and revive prior learning but also to transform and transfer it into a range of new and different guises. This is what Bjork calls 'varying'.[3] Through these key activities, and with the added levers of choice and challenge, we can support pupils to develop greater mastery, confidence and ownership of their learning. What a great recipe for revitalising revision – and how reassuring for busy teachers to be able to periodically check that learning can be successfully recalled from long-term memory and is not merely evidence of temporary performance.

Importantly, these techniques provide teachers with regular, ongoing and specific formative assessment opportunities, from which they can plan necessary interventions. For example, if certain pupils cannot recall the number bonds to 10, or the key events leading up to the Second World War, then this would become an obvious focus for reteaching.

---

1 https://bjorklab.psych.ucla.edu/research/#interleaving.
2 https://bjorklab.psych.ucla.edu/research/#ntd.
3 https://bjorklab.psych.ucla.edu/research/#ibdd.

Watch out for when the lamp is switched back on!

Exploit the excitement and anticipation

Finally, the fact that the prompts are dangling from the ceiling, or hidden in sealed containers labelled with a large question mark, helps to intrigue and tantalise the pupils. In addition, as they glint in the sunlight or flicker in the breeze, these resources remind teachers of the prior learning that may be ready for revisiting. Better still, they can be called upon at a moment's notice and when pupils least expect it.

Principles to underpin your practice

> Increase the frequency and status of revision by keeping the evidence of prior learning in your and your pupils' eyeline.

> Treat your ceiling as prime untapped display space. Make a virtue of the fact that it is not as easily accessible and therefore not subject to frequent change. Use this space for the most significant, overarching aspects of your curriculum (as we discussed in relation to the Pareto principle in the introduction).

> Information needs to travel from the ceiling directly into active learning and back again.

Practical techniques

Finding prominent spaces to store prior learning

We know from the work of Robert Bjork and others that distributed practice, or spacing, is one of the most robust, effective ways of improving learning. However, spacing calls for intervals of time in-between exposures. During these intervals, ensure that elements of pupils' previous work are placed strategically around your classroom in order to facilitate the techniques in this chapter.

Hidden in Plain Sight. Retain evidence of prior learning and store this in prominent places within the classroom. Cardboard tubes or large plastic jars are ideal for this purpose. Discuss with the pupils what label, symbol or image could be used to represent the contents and stick this onto your vessel.

The idea is that pupils should be able to see the stimulus but not interact with it, at least not yet. Increase the intrigue, perhaps by using a large label that says, 'Do not touch … yet!' This develops a culture where pupils are routinely asked, 'What can you remember about what we put in the jar?' (Or tube, rocket, secret scroll or whatever your preferred storage method is.) 'Can anyone remember anything from our earlier learning that might be useful in our

current work?' Not only does this kind of memory challenge help to keep pupils engaged with prior learning but it also serves to deepen their understanding.

Make this even more memorable by 'capturing' evidence of learning in an interactive way. For example, crowdsourcing is a fabulously versatile activity in which pupils are asked to anonymously record a significant idea on a piece of paper that they then scrunch up into a 'snowball' and throw into the centre of the room. Pupils can take a selection of snowballs, working collaboratively to verify and strengthen the ideas, before symbolically capturing the very best in the snowball container.

At strategic points, this learning can then be resurrected and revived. Before opening the snowball container, you could start the process off by asking questions like:

> What do you still feel confident about?

> What needs revisiting?

> What new learning could you add now?

> What questions would you ask now?

Secret Scrolls. A variation on the previous technique would be to use a set of scrolls to record the evidence of prior learning and store these in a corner of the room. They could be heaped together or stored in a chicken-wire cage or appropriately labelled box. The main difference here is that, just like in an ancient library, the scrolls can store a lot of information and be examined in any order. The idea of processing, ordering and making connections between the information contained can be exploited to increase engagement.

 Rolling Up and Rolling Out. Throughout this book, we describe ways of capturing learning using large rolls of paper to create easily stored records of pupils' best work at a specific time. Indeed, this is very much like a super-sized version of a secret scroll, and can be ceremonially placed in a 'cupboard of excellence', or similar. You could even store this in your Cabinet of Curiosities (see Chapter 1). Reintroduce the exemplars periodically to check whether learning is still live – for example, by asking, 'What can we remember about the learning before we unroll the paper and look at it again?', 'Well done, we have remembered most of this but what did we forget?', 'How shall we go over this again?' Encourage pupils to add new learning to the scrolls, ideally in a different colour to demonstrate progress over time. Redisplaying this work helps to consolidate the key learning throughout the year and can also make for very dynamic revision and transition activities.

 Stepping Back in Time. Stepping stones are large pieces of paper scribed with a challenge or prompt that are placed on the floor, and we'll go on to explore these in more detail in Chapter 3. You can store them in large mystery folders or envelopes and label each with an intriguing question mark. As with the snowballs and secret scrolls, hide these 'in plain sight'. Again, create the expectation that pupils will be revisiting their prior learning in an engaging and memorable way – but they won't know exactly when. For instance,

at unexpected moments, invite pupils to choose one of the mystery envelopes and reveal the stepping stones once again (see Chapter 3 for different activities using these).

Hibernation. This celebrates the ceremonial taking down and storing of the current displays ready for reactivating – and for pupils to demonstrate deep learning by teaching the content to others – at some point in the future. Think about how pupils can be actively involved in the process through discussion – for example, 'What are you sure that you have remembered/totally understood?', 'What could you confidently teach somebody else?' and, crucially, 'What do you need me to recap with you before we put this learning into hibernation?'

Using the ceiling as 'cloud storage'

Create symbolic moments when the class agrees that learning is secure and ready to be sent up to 'the cloud' for storage. This puts a physical distance between the learners and the learning but creates a constant reminder for them, and for you as the teacher. It reaffirms pupils' understanding that content is going to be pulled back into the learning arena to check what they can recall.

Build up the feeling of anticipation by telling your pupils that sometime soon the stored learning will be unleashed. Then reintroduce and revise the learning from the ceiling. You might try inviting a VIP – for example, the head teacher, another teacher or a visitor – to ceremonially bring down the learning

stores. Having a visitor do this heightens both the significance and memorability of the event. An added advantage is that the VIP can engage in discussion with the pupils, possibly inviting them to teach him or her.

Creative variations on this premise might include:

Memory Mobiles. How about using attractive mobiles to actively challenge memory later in the learning? Or using washing lines in a new way to symbolically represent key learning points in the form of cryptic coded clues rather than obvious cues?

Case study

Clearly challenging

In an MFL lesson, the teacher had set up a washing line across the classroom but had adapted it by attaching clear plastic envelopes. These contained extra challenges which she could use for easily differentiated extension tasks. The transparency of the envelopes meant that she could choose how much of the challenge to make visible as an intriguing tantaliser, or to give pupils a glimpse of a more difficult challenge that they might want to attempt.

 **Tasty Tacos.** Give individual pupils or groups a paper plate which they can fold in half and use to contain information about a topic that they have recently studied. Encourage them to adopt a 'confetti' approach to the filling and to incorporate a mix of questions, tasks, clues, riddles, images, etc. Many schools now use versions of a 'chilli challenge' where pupils can self-select the level of challenge denoted by the heat rating. Invite them to make some of their taco fillings 'super spicy' and challenging, perhaps signifying this by using different colour-coding. Sealing the crimped edges with staples traps the contents securely. Leaving a small gap between the staples means you can thread through string to suspend them with, and allows you to insert extra ideas or teacher challenges. An alternative to Tasty Tacos could be for pupils to construct polyhedral nets – of their own design or using a template – onto which they write key points, words, questions, etc. Next, these could be filled with additional information and detail before finally being assembled to form the solid shape.

▲ **Take Down the Tacos.** Invite pupils to work together to tackle the learning challenges contained inside the taco shells. Groups could take on the tacos that they initially created and reflect on what they have learned in the meantime, or you could mix this up and give everyone a taco created by someone else. In the latter case, you could include an opportunity for the groups to present their ideas to the tacos' creators for critique and feedback.

Case study: The Dearne ALC

Maximising mock exam feedback

We saw an interesting combination of the Tasty Tacos and Message to Myself techniques in Joanne's English lesson with a Year 11 class. It was a revision session based on the GCSE non-fiction paper. This was a tricky time of year, and could have been a difficult lesson in which to get pupils engaged. However, Joanne was able to capitalise on her excellent, good-humoured relationship with the class and tackle the analysis of mark allocation and individual areas for improvement in an engaging and memorable way.

Just prior to the lesson, Joanne draped a length of string around the outside edges of the tables, which were grouped in a horseshoe formation. When pupils entered they were confronted with the string and a paper plate on each of their tables, which prompted a great deal of curiosity about the connection between these seemingly random objects and about what might happen next.

Joanne then invited pupils to review all the different sources of feedback they had been given during their recent exam practice and to distil this onto one piece of A4 paper. After being given time to do this, the pupils were invited to fold the paper plate in half, thus creating their own Tasty Taco, and to conceal their personal feedback record inside. Joanne likened

these tacos to the concept of the Horcrux in the Harry Potter series: a significant piece of themselves that could be retrieved later.

The final stage involved pupils being challenged to label the outside of their tacos not with their name but with a symbol that captured the most important feedback message they had received. One pupil commented, 'This helped me because now I will easily remember what I need to do in the exam. I will keep looking at the picture. The symbol really made me think about what was the most important thing.' It was genuinely

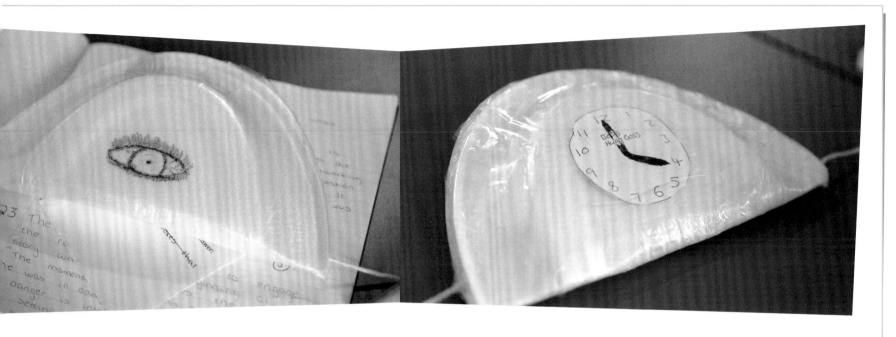

moving to see the range of creative depictions generated by these adolescent pupils. They included a crown – 'Because I am great and I now just need to believe in myself' – and a potato waffle – 'Because I need to stop waffling and get to the point more quickly in my answers!'

Finally, pupils linked their tacos together using the string, an activity which generated a great deal of discussion about the meaning of the symbols. An added by-product of this discussion was that pupils reiterated their key feedback message several times to different people, thus helping to lock it more

firmly in their memories. The memorability was further enhanced by involving pupils in the act of hoisting up the strings of tacos, and by the fact that they would remain prominently displayed until nearer the exam. Having the tacos on display, but out of reach, meant that Joanne could routinely refer to them as part of ongoing learning and revision – for example, by asking, 'Charlie, what does your symbol mean? Can you recall three key messages you wrote to yourself before we unleash the tacos and open them to check?'

Message to Myself. Have your pupils write a letter, or produce a blog or vlog for their 'future self' to open at a significant time. You could do this shortly after mocks, two months before final exams, or at the end of Year 6 ready for the transition to secondary in September. A red postbox, made out of a cardboard box and situated somewhere prominent, could work brilliantly here and allow pupils to post additional memos to themselves. Keep engagement and motivation high by periodically challenging pupils to recall what advice from their past selves is contained in their letter, blog or vlog.

Bunting. Use bunting made from plain triangular cards on which pupils write three key points, words, questions or answers (one along each of the edges) at the end of a topic. This activity really comes to life when pupils circulate to challenge each other to tessellate their triangles. 'I have a question/technical term. Does your triangle contain the answer/definition?' When the pupils have managed to link the triangles, explain that they will be strung up as bunting. However, make it clear that at some point in future it will be cut down so they can see how well they have remembered the learning by linking it up again. Extend the challenge when the bunting is released by asking your pupils to not only link the triangles but to use the ideas and concepts as prompts to create detailed sentences or paragraphs that sum up the core learning.

● Metacognition and self-regulated learning | Emotional engagement ▲ Retrieval and revision

Space Rocket. Work with pupils to create and fill a space rocket, or time capsule, with different evidence of their learning, which could take the form of audio and video recordings, pieces of writing, drawings, artefacts and photographs. Do this at the consolidation stage of the learning process, perhaps playing up the fact that they are ready to 'take off with' or 'launch' their learning. Attach string or transparent fishing line to the rocket and then hoist it up using a previously placed hook (this can be in the ceiling or high on a wall). Secure the free end of the line to another hook that's placed within reach. It can then be brought down with a theatrical countdown for reentry into the classroom prior to revisiting. Pupils routinely comment on the fact that this makes revision more exciting and memorable.

Paper Chains. These are an easy way to involve pupils in recording important elements of learning and exploring potential links between them. Different-coloured paper strips could be used strategically to create the paper chains. In the case of MFL, each colour could denote a different part of speech, perhaps linked (or rearranged later) to form grammatically correct sentences. Consider what you could use colour-coding to represent in your own subject or classroom.

You could try incorporating a competitive element by dividing the class into teams to see who can:

> Create the most challenging or imaginative set of links based on any aspect of the term's learning.

> Create the longest paper chain the quickest, perhaps beginning in opposite corners of the room. Increase the levels of ownership and thinking by stipulating that once a word has been added to the chain any pupil in that team can be challenged, by the teacher or by the opposing team, to demonstrate their understanding of it. In our MFL example, this could be to either give a correct translation of the word or use it correctly in a sentence.

Reintroduce the paper chains by unleashing them from the ceiling and inviting pupils to carefully disconnect them. Next, ask them to make something new from the paper strips – for example, put them together to develop full sentences or paragraphs.

▲ **Lucky Dip.** Use strong, transparent fishing line to hang up a colourful, opened umbrella by its handle and use it to store snippets of current learning, but only when the class have agreed they all feel secure and confident about it. Later, have a lucky dip into the umbrella to pull out a prompt which can be used to revisit prior learning. Alternatively, you could close the umbrella, ready to open at some point in the future. In this instance, once opened you could scatter the contents like confetti for pupils to discuss, explore and organise. The fishing line can be attached to the ceiling using metal or plastic hooks. These could also be suspended from a washing line that has been fixed across the classroom if the ceiling cannot be used.

Case study: Hoyland Common Primary

Tessellating triangles

We worked with Rosie to introduce the triangle bunting activity with her Year 3 class in their geography lesson. This slotted in easily mid-way through the teaching sequence, acting as a mini-plenary, and allowed Rosie to ascertain whether previous learning was still live. Pupils worked in pairs to generate a question, a keyword and a symbol, all related to the topic of rivers. This activity required pupils to work collaboratively, to practise and revive key vocabulary and to decide which aspects were the most important to question. Because Rosie was not trapped in delivery mode, she was more able to give 'process praise' and subtly intervene to unearth any misconceptions and gaps in pupils' understanding. Once they had finalised their three items, these were written along the edges of the card triangles.

Finally, pupils circulated around the room, challenging each other to see if they could link their triangles in any way. 'Does your word answer our question?' 'I think your symbol represents a stream. We have that word on this edge here. They can join up.'

As a reward for letting us take photos of them at work, and so missing their regular break time, the class had been given a slightly extended break. The pupils' engagement with their learning and motivation was wonderfully illustrated when we overheard a group of boys saying, 'If we stay in for ten minutes, we can find the other answers and join up our triangles and we'll still get some break time because we've got extra!' It's not often you see a learning challenge 'top-trumping' a game of football, is it?

⬤ Metacognition and self-regulated learning | Emotional engagement ▲ Retrieval and revision

Balloon Burst. Suspend a net from the ceiling and fill this with balloons containing messages, challenges or instructions; these could be hidden inside on strips of paper or written on the surface. At a strategic point, after building sufficient interest and anticipation, it's time for them to be released. Imagine the excitement of pupils as they work to discover what is contained in, or written on, the balloons. Depending on what you are teaching, the content might range from high-frequency words for Year 1 to exam questions for an A-level class, but the engagement will be the same.

Helium Hideaway. Hide symbols, questions or keywords inside helium balloons. You could allow them to rise to the ceiling or use weights to set them at different heights, or achieve a similar effect by varying the amount of helium you add. You may want to attach a label with instructions or extra information to the end of the string. The joy of this technique is that the balloons will deflate slowly and gradually descend back into the midst of other learning activities. Rather than being a distraction, we can exploit pupils' excitement as they watch and start to anticipate the next new challenge.

Brag Tags. These are wristbands that can be made from strips of paper or card, whilst pre-made versions can be purchased cheaply online. These are useful in many different educational ways. We were initially inspired by Paul Dix's idea of using wristbands to give pupils feedback and targets

 Responsive teaching  Oracy and 'word wealth' Collaborative learning

(see Dix, 2017). We have developed this approach further by using the bands within classroom displays, specifically to aid revision, once they have served their active purpose on pupils' wrists. One very effective approach involves writing personalised targets or challenges on a pupil's wristband. This prompts parents and, indeed, other pupils and teachers to ask the pupil about what is written there, thus keeping learning visible and live. Obviously, the language is important here: phrases such as 'Ask me about …' or 'I can now …' keep the tone positive and celebratory. With older pupils, we've seen teachers exploiting the idea of festival wristbands, with all their associated kudos, to great effect.

Only when the pupil can prove that they have completed the challenge or mastered the target can the band be removed. The wristbands now become 'brag tags'; evidence of their new skills and knowledge and reminders of the challenges they have overcome.

Case study

Language links

In this Key Stage 4 MFL lesson, the teacher and pupils had worked together to build a particularly vibrant display area. The walls were festooned with paper chains, with each learning link containing a keyword in the target language on one side and the English translation on the reverse. The teacher commented that, in this instance, 'The walls just seemed more accessible for the pupils than the ceiling– and I want them to refer to the paper chains more regularly than I first planned.'

Pupils certainly seemed to be doing exactly that, and were adding new vocabulary to the chains. However, this was done with the caveat that they could only add a word when they felt confident about how to use it correctly – and could demonstrate this. Pupils were also routinely returning to the paper chains to check or retrieve vocabulary when they needed it in the lesson.

 Linking the Brag Tags. Rather than waste these brag tags, encourage pupils to keep them, linking them together to form chains that will grow as their learning develops. Like the paper chains mentioned earlier, these can be hung from the ceiling and reintroduced and re-explored to check pupils' recall. For example, 'Can you still write a great sentence with a capital letter, full stop and finger spaces?' or 'Can you still describe the process of osmosis?'

 Brag Tags Bonanza. At appropriate times, encourage pupils to work in groups to connect all of the tags they have accumulated between them, with the stipulation that the group must discuss and agree what links can be made. This could be followed by the ceremonial linking of the tags collected by the whole class. 'What goes with what?' 'We are trying to get from one side of the classroom to the other. Who has a new brag tag they could put up?' 'You can't add one unless you can *prove* that you understand it.'

Case study: Kirk Balk Secondary

Remember then reassemble

The Year 9 classroom was festooned with evidence of prior learning, captured in the form of pupil-generated colour-coded questions and answers which had been written onto paper chains and assembled in a random order before 'sending them soaring'. The pupils had remained curious about these paper chains and, over the course of several lessons, repeatedly asked what they were going to be used for. The teacher, Lynne, simply told them they'd have to 'wait and see', to keep their interest piqued. This was the lesson when they would finally find out.

The teacher announced that it was time to 'unleash the learning' by pulling down the paper chains. The class unanimously volunteered one of the taller pupils for the job. When the paper chains fell onto the desks, pupils instinctively began to grab and claim sections. This led neatly to the teacher's next challenge: namely to dismantle the chains carefully and to work collaboratively to match the questions with the correct answers. It was interesting to see how the pupils immediately began to discuss the questions and speculate about the potential answers. Very soon a good-natured competition arose and pupils started to search out the correct answers with more urgency in an attempt to make the most links in the allocated time. The teacher commented that they had stayed focused and had been confidently using key terminology which they would normally find difficult to remember.

Case study: Darton College

Grabbing hold of the knowledge

Amie was delivering an art lesson with a Year 8 nurture group who had been learning about the landscape artist Henri Rousseau. The challenge here was in authentically getting the Dynamically Different Classroom Project techniques into the lesson with discernment for the complex needs of this group, who were some of the school's most vulnerable learners. In Amie's words:

> There was a lot of 'below the tip of the iceberg' planning that went into this one. Would the sound of the balloons bursting scare them? Would they be able to touch the balloons? Would it be too overstimulating for them?

With these potential barriers in mind, Amie met with the learners before the lesson to discuss what she had planned and find out the answers to her questions. The pupils discussed all the proposed techniques and decided that these sounded OK; they wouldn't mind balloons being burst, but only if they were told when it was going to happen.

Amie and a colleague then set about creating an immersive experience from the moment the group entered the classroom. They walked through a doorway covered in overgrown

vines to the sound of a tropical storm playing through the projector. Amie had written keywords on labels and tied these to balloons. Information on the labels included the name of the artist, the name of the painting, descriptive words and dates, and this began a knowledge-gathering exercise. Some words were relevant but not all of them.

● Metacognition and self-regulated learning | Emotional engagement ▲ Retrieval and revision

When the pupils came in, the balloons were suspended from the ceiling in a net and these were released at an appropriate moment early in the lesson. The pupils had to grab a balloon and work collaboratively to decide whether or not their label described Rousseau's painting *Tiger in a Tropical Storm*. If they decided they had 'grabbed some knowledge' they wrote it on their 'Wonder Wall': the display they used to share their wonderful learning. Amie also used the Helium Hideaway technique as an extension to the knowledge-gathering exercise, by setting helium balloons at different heights with instructions on luggage tags attached to the strings.

The main learning phase asked pupils to use the knowledge they had collected to create a collaborative piece of art in the style of Rousseau. Amie had set up learning stations around the classroom and learners opted into their preferred task; choosing to produce either a stormy sky, an animal stalking its way through the jungle looking for its prey, or a tropical jungle backdrop filled with exotic flowers and plants.

The resulting display demonstrated the learning and also transformed the classroom into a place they could call theirs in the future lessons they would spend there. Amie summed up what she felt had been the impact of the lesson:

> *It was meaningful. It was beautiful. It was a celebration of their knowledge. I know that the learning that happened was important and that we all felt something special.*

Treasure Hunt. Use your ceiling to display a revision treasure hunt. Use transparent fishing line attached to hooks in the ceiling, or washing lines strung across the room, to hang up large-scale card prompts. These could include questions, key vocabulary, pictures or symbols relating to a topic. Challenge pupils to navigate a route through by connecting one to another. Although the display remains static it can be used dynamically by asking pupils to plot different routes through on different occasions – for example, by creating different rules, such as 'You must find links to move diagonally across the classroom', 'Your route needs to include at least three symbols, and you need to explain how these link to the topic'. If appropriate, you could provide a treasure chest full of fun activities, puzzles, code-breaking games, etc. that pupils can select from when they've completed the treasure hunt.

Significant Symbols. Hang up symbols or pictures connected to important aspects of the current learning. This is another way to keep the learning 'simmering' as, at any time, individuals or pairs of pupils can be set challenges of identification, classification or selection, which they respond to by going and standing under the corresponding symbol. These are called GAS (go and stand) activities and they are a quick way of taking a measure of the whole class' understanding as each pupil's physical position demonstrates their answer, which can then be unpicked through questioning.

● Metacognition and self-regulated learning ┃ Emotional engagement ▲ Retrieval and revision

Case study

GAS – Go and Stand

In one design and technology lesson we hung up cardboard versions of various tools all around the classroom. Pupils knew that they might be called upon to go and stand under the correct tool when given instructions or asked questions like: 'Go and stand under the saw that you'd use for making accurate straight cuts in small pieces of wood', 'Which is the coping saw?', 'What would you use for cutting curved lines in plastics?' In another lesson we used symbols from an electrical circuit in a similar way.

Umbrella Questioning. Thread fishing line through the top of an opened umbrella (you could use a needle or cut a small hole in the fabric) and suspend it from the ceiling with the handle pointing down. Attach questions to the spokes. If you use a traditional umbrella, the curved hook is an ideal place for pupils to attach their answers, key information or further questions.

Overarching Umbrellas. Use several different-coloured umbrellas to represent the main overarching component parts of your curriculum or exam specification. Examples could include: medieval medicine and Nazi Germany in history; spelling, punctuation and grammar (SPaG), reading comprehension and maths for Key Stage 2; Year 6 SATs; or early learning goals. The size and vibrancy of the umbrellas themselves act as a striking reminder of the vital, overarching elements of study whilst the different colours can help as a memory aid.

As part of the revision process, pose the question, 'If you were asked about this tomorrow (or if the exam was brought forward), which component do you currently feel least confident about?' Ask pupils to stand beneath the umbrella which represents that component. Challenge the pupils standing under each umbrella to work as a group to articulate everything they know about that particular topic before going back to check their notes for anything that they may have missed during their discussion. This is also an easy way to generate differentiated groups for subsequent work and responsive reteaching as necessary, as the pupils clustered under each umbrella will have the same self-perceived weaknesses.

Ceiling Circuits. Use the different-coloured umbrellas as described in Overarching Umbrellas, but instead assign a task, question or activity to each to create a circuit training course. You can leave the umbrellas up but keep varying the tasks and topics. At appropriate times during the learning, organise the pupils into groups who will rotate around the umbrella stations at a given signal, saying as much as they can within the time limit you give them. The collaborative aspect, plus the variety of topics and requirement to work hard for short periods of time with regular breaks and transitions, is particularly motivating for many pupils.

Case study: Hoyland Common Primary

Under my umbrella

As we saw in the case studies in Chapter 1, Rosie had set out to maximise the potential of all of her display space. Even the ceiling had been utilised as a prompt for the pupils to interact with the learning they would be doing in their main topic of rivers. Rosie had suspended an umbrella from the ceiling and pupils used various symbols to articulate their thoughts:

> **Sun.** Tell me something that you already know about our topic, something that you know is accurate and that a peer could learn from.

> **Cloud.** What are you looking forward to during our topic? Or is there something that you want to study or learn about over the next half term?

> **Raindrop.** Do you have a question about our topic that you'd like to know the answer to?

It was interesting to see how pairs and small groups of children gathered under the umbrella at various times to add their own ideas and to discuss comments already hanging there.

And What Else?

> ....

> ....

> ....

> ....

> ....

> ....

> ....

> ....

> ....

> ....

> ....

> ....

■ Responsive teaching ● Oracy and 'word wealth' ● Collaborative learning

Chapter 3

FLOORS: NOT JUST FOR STANDING OR SITTING ON

In this chapter

We encourage you to think about the untapped potential of your floor space. The floor is a large area which can provide opportunities for pupils to move away from the constraints of their desks. Using deliberate movement to punctuate your lessons at significant points both boosts engagement and re-energises pupils, as well as giving their brains an oxygen boost (Jensen, 2005). Crucially, these bursts of activity function as significant memory markers, making them an important and strategic tool for keeping learning live.

Sound familiar?

When was the last time you thought about the floor in your classroom? Beyond noticing wayward litter or lost property, chances are you might not have given it much specific thought, and why would you? However, we would argue that this is a sizeable area to explore – both literally and metaphorically. Your floor might not physically be as large as you would like but it serves several very important functions, the potential of which might be going untapped. The floor:

> Allows pupils – and teachers – to move.

> Provides a foundation on which all learning stands. It is a literal underpinning that can be built on.

Floors are so mundane it is perhaps unsurprising that they are largely ignored. However, let's consider the symbolic connotations for a moment. For example, 'having the floor' is not just the act of talking. There is a performance and, indeed, a status element at play here; giving someone the floor means we are offering them our respect and attention. The default in the classroom is for the teacher to hold the floor, with many lessons dominated by teacher input. Teachers take for granted their automatic right to move freely around the classroom, but why not the pupils? As presenters, we cannot deliver our message effectively without wandering around the space. We think as we move, and we speak as we think.

It is interesting to note that teachers will often cite nursery and reception-aged children as the most self-directing and inquisitive learners. Much of this may be due to the fact that they are given a diet of exploration and choice through continuous provision. They are free to venture in and out of the home corner, relax in the reading zone or move outside for activities in the fresh air.

Continuous provision tends to disappear as pupils age and move up through the school years. External forces may have conditioned teachers to set up their classrooms in a particular way without ever really questioning why. Why does continuous provision tend to disappear at the end of reception? Why don't we see Year 6 pupils routinely selecting their own learning tasks, methods and places of learning?

We do realise, of course, that sometimes the most appropriate place for learning is at a table. Indeed, we want to give pupils a stable base and provide the classroom with a conventional sense of structure. However, much of our thinking about the classroom layout will have been shaped by the approximately 10,500 hours that we have spent in the classroom as pupils ourselves; they have given us a subconscious blueprint. It is now for us to consider whether this blueprint is in keeping with today's modern learner and with our own evolving philosophy of teaching and learning.

So what needs to happen?

Give pupils opportunities to move away from the constraints of their tables

We know that pupils learn particularly effectively when they are actively and physically engaged in their learning (Jensen, 2005). Through movement they are building muscle memory, and we can exploit that much more effectively in classrooms. Our experience has always been that by adding more active opportunities and creating a truly collaborative, immersive and sensory experience the activity itself becomes more profound, enjoyable and memorable.

Repurpose and reinvent the floor space in different ways on different days

Pupils have a set of expectations each time they step into our classrooms. Sometimes it can be very powerful to subvert the expectation as an immediate way of engaging all learners. Whilst teenagers may posture and feign indifference, they still fundamentally need and respond to variety and intrigue. Nobody is ever too old to be surprised or excited!

Equally important is the fact that we are living in rapidly changing times, so the classroom should be an important training ground for fostering skills such as adaptability. Routines are something of a double-edged sword: whilst they can be very useful as administrative tools, they can also be a hindrance by establishing a comfort zone. By training our pupils to 'expect the unexpected' we can prevent them from settling into passive complacency.

Principles to underpin your practice

› Movement aids memorability and facilitates muscle memory, particularly when used in conjunction with a rhythm. For some pupils with SEND, movement can be a useful way to re-energise, and to turn around a counterproductive mental state. For example, incorporating

slower movement can be useful in calming down overactive pupils and thus support better concentration.

> Movement can be used to deliberately punctuate and emphasise key moments within a learning sequence.

> Movement re-energises pupils in a meaningful way when coupled with the powerful pedagogical techniques described here.

> Working on the floor positions pupils closer to their work, allowing them to expand, be surrounded by and physically immersed in their learning with minimally invasive teacher input.

> Working on the floor positions pupils physically closer to each other, helping to encourage improved interpersonal and communication skills by removing physical barriers.

> Working on the floor is more natural and comfortable. Pupils can readily shift their position and get comfortable – which is, of course, one of the more basic elements of Maslow's hierarchy of needs.

Many schools are already engaging with programmes such as Kinetic Letters, which involves pupils lying on their tummies on the floor for most reading and writing activities, especially during the foundation stage.[1] The thinking here is that a strong pelvic girdle enables children to sit still and concentrate without wriggling, and this can be strengthened by working on the floor initially (Williamson and Wilson, 2012: 2.16).

---

1 www.kineticletters.co.uk.

However, do not assume that the benefits are confined only to our younger learners. Did you know that several famous writers, including Mark Twain and Truman Capote, always wrote whilst lying down? For pupils with certain learning or developmental difficulties, writing in this position may be helpful in terms of allowing them to concentrate totally on the writing process rather than expend energy on sitting appropriately.

Practical techniques

Entrances and exits

Entering and exiting the classroom can be mundane, barely registering in the consciousness of our pupils. This is particularly true for secondary school pupils, who visit a myriad of classrooms in a typical week. Use the moment of entry to set the tone for your lesson and the learning that is to follow. The techniques that follow also ensure that not a second of learning time is wasted, as pupils are engaged and challenged from the very outset.

⬤ Metacognition and self-regulated learning ❘ Emotional engagement ▲ Retrieval and revision

Crossing the Threshold. Make more of the moment when your pupils first step into your learning environment by placing a large-scale stimulus just inside the doorway. This stimulus could be:

> A learning objective or lesson focus.

> An intriguing image.

> A question.

> A keyword.

> A provocative statement.

> A clue.

> An incomplete statement, sentence or word.

> An affirmation or inspirational mantra.

> Anything else you can think of?

You can vary the instruction and follow-up task – for example, 'Memorise what you have just read', 'Discuss this with a partner when you sit down' or 'Respond verbally as you step over the threshold'. This final variant, in particular, is effective as a pre-assessment activity as it can be used to gauge levels of prior knowledge and understanding – for example, by asking pupils to state whether they 'don't know this/are not sure/know this'. Or you could use one of the many coded systems for declaring understanding, such as the RAG (red, amber, green) rating.

The threshold activity effectively sets the tone and expectations for what is to follow. This does away with the need for low-level settling activities and eradicates any 'lost time' as pupils are immediately immersed in the learning challenge: you start as you mean to go on. For older learners – who are constantly moving between different classrooms, teachers, subjects and expectations – this is a particularly powerful transition strategy, as it hooks them into the ethos of each classroom immediately.

Repeat the process as pupils exit the classroom and ensure that they 'check out' of your lesson in a meaningful way. This time you could:

> Change the stimulus based on how the learning has progressed.

> Use the original stimulus but add sentence stems or thinking routines to encourage progression – for example, 'I now think …', 'I now know …', etc.

> Turn the stimulus upside down, or cover it up, and challenge pupils to recall as much detail as they can.

> Anything else you can think of?

Case study: St Luke's Primary

Going over high-frequency words

The reception classroom at St Luke's contains three doors: one leading into the corridor, another giving access to the outdoor area and the third to the adjoining classroom space. Pupils are used to free flow in their learning and enter and exit through each doorway multiple times each day.

On the threshold of each door, the teachers, Sue and Tommie, had taped a large sheet of paper with a keyword written across it in large bold writing. The expectation was that pupils would read, and ideally say, the word as they stepped over it. What began as an engaging learning game quickly became habitual. Because vocabulary is so important at this early stage of learning, Sue and Tommie noted that it was very useful for the pupils to, 'Keep going over it, literally and mentally!'

Step Back in Time. Adapt the threshold idea to create a highly effective revision activity. Ensure that the stimulus placed on the threshold relates to prior learning and challenges pupils to be ready to articulate what they can remember about it after they have entered the classroom. They can indicate their degree of confidence using sentence stems, such as 'I remember …', 'I think …' or 'I'm not completely sure, but …'

Threshold Tombola. Maximise the moment when pupils enter your classroom further still by meeting them at the door and inviting them to select from a tombola-like tub. By using this method of random selection you can assign tasks or groupings that will be important later in the lesson.

Different variations could include:

> Inviting pupils to each pull out a raffle ticket. Use the numbering to determine groupings, activities or different working zones in the classroom.

> Replacing the raffle tickets with mystery envelopes or mini gift-wrapped objects that can be opened at strategic times to introduce new elements to the learning.

> Filling the tombola tub with clues or questions relating to prior learning. At random moments pupils can ask their question or offer their clue and challenge the rest of the class to prove that their learning is still live. Make this more powerfully playful by having pupils compete to talk about their answer for a specified amount of time, perhaps by adopting the style and rules of the Radio 4 programme *Just a Minute*.

Metacognition and self-regulated learning | Emotional engagement ▲ Retrieval and revision

Case study: St Luke's Primary

Threshold objectives

In many schools, lesson objectives are typically written on the whiteboard ready to be copied by the pupils as a kind of settling activity. Teachers often comment on the fact that, whilst they know they are expected to display the lesson objective, this copying process is neither challenging nor engaging for the pupils.

Katherine, a Year 4 teacher at St Luke's, was keen to work with us to explore how to use a threshold activity to encourage pupils to consciously engage with the lesson objective. We wrote it on a large sheet of paper and taped it onto the doorway floor. Pupils were greeted in the corridor and responded with genuine enthusiasm to the news that there would be a 'threshold memory challenge'.

The subsequent instruction was for pupils to enter the classroom quietly, read the objective – which, as an added test, was missing a keyword – then make their way to their seats and copy the objective into their books from memory. The additional challenge was to predict the missing word.

Pupils responded with energy and focus, becoming quite competitive to see who could write the objective down correctly first. Pupils were so engaged, a spontaneous debate regarding the missing word broke out prior to the teacher revealing the complete objective.

Finally, when pupils left the classroom they were confronted by the threshold question, 'What was today's lesson objective?' This effectively challenged their memories and meant they were still discussing the learning as they walked out for morning break.

Powerful perimeters

You can also use the readily available space at the outer edges of your classroom much more dynamically by adopting some of the following strategies.

 Memory March. Challenge pupils to move purposefully around the periphery whilst chanting the most significant message from the lesson or topic. Obviously, we are not advocating a full-scale return to learning by rote; this is not the mindless chanting of yesteryear! Instead, we would suggest constantly refreshing this approach by adding different background music, adjusting the beat, rhythm or tempo, swapping direction or simply changing the way that pupils move. Once again, keep the tone and the energy powerfully playful.

▲ **Sweeping Glance.** Invite pupils to take a brisk but purposeful walk around the perimeter of the classroom, perhaps accompanied by a countdown, whilst surveying what's on the walls (this could include adaptations to displays as described in Chapter 1). Once they are back at their tables, follow this with a memory challenge.

Stop and Take Stock. This is a variant of Sweeping Glance with the added expectation that pupils must physically stop whenever they encounter something that they find difficult to understand or remember. The teacher's key role here is to note the points where individual pupils are stopping and struggling. This activity works diagnostically to expose aspects that need reteaching. Make this activity more powerful by stipulating that pupils can help each other to keep moving forward by teaching one another when they become stuck.

Thinking Circuits. Place a trail of tantalising and related items – such as objects, questions, statements, artefacts, etc. – around the edges of the classroom and invite pupils to walk around the circuit, thinking about:

› How the things are connected.

› If there are any odd ones out (you could place some red herrings in the mix).

› What the learning objective might be.

› How the circuit might link to prior learning. (Here you could use prompts such as 'What topic does this remind you of?')

› Anything else you can think of?

This activity has the benefit of settling pupils into their learning but stimulating their thinking at the same time: a tricky combination to achieve, which goes far beyond the remit of traditional settling activities. This would work particularly well at the start of a lesson, when returning from lunch or break or at transitional points in a learning sequence.

Enhance the activity further by taking a multisensory approach and using varied stimuli that involve as many senses as possible at the same time. This creates an enriched experience, hopefully leading to deeper learning.

GAS (Go and Stand). We have adapted this idea from the 'Go And See' investigative concept suggested by Steve Bowkett et al. (2007: 28). Place items, questions, images, problems or artefacts in the corners of the room and ask pupils to stand next to the one which they:

› Think is correct (in the context of the question you've posed).

› Think is most interesting.

› Find most challenging (we need to train them to walk past anything easy).

This strategy is about choice: committing to a position and owning it. Ensure that you invite pupils to explain or justify their choice. An extension could be for pupils to try to persuade others to change their opinion and move to a different physical position.

An added advantage here is the diagnostic element that helps the teacher shape future learning. For example, how many pupils have identified the correct answer and were able to articulate and develop it? Does this reveal any particular misconceptions? Pupils' choices can also be used to generate groupings for follow-up activities. 'Can everyone standing next to choice A turn over that piece of paper to reveal your group's task?'

Moving in the middle

Stepping Stones. Use large, colourful sheets of paper to display questions, facts, images, tasks, etc. all linked to a particular topic. Place these randomly around the floor. The idea is for pupils to interact with these prompts by moving amongst them. This can be used as a knowledge-gathering or knowledge-testing exercise. Variations could include:

> Challenging pupils to visit as many stepping stones as possible in a given time. If they know the answer to the question, they can move on. If they are unsure, they must stay on that 'stone' until a peer can help them become unstuck by

teaching them. The teacher can ensure accountability by stipulating that they may spot-check understanding at any time by pausing the activity and asking random pupils to explain the answer to the stepping stone they have just moved on from.

> Increasing the mystery. Begin by placing the stepping stones upside down, then play some appropriate music and when the music stops, pupils must turn over the stone and discuss it with the people closest to them at the time.

Case study: Convent of Jesus and Mary RC Infant School and Nursery

Tiger feet

In the autumn term of Year 1, Debora, the class teacher, used Stepping Stones to check that the children could sequence the story of *The Tiger Who Came to Tea* by Judith Kerr. As these young children were very early readers, she cut out colour pictures of main parts of the story and stuck them onto paper to form the stepping stones. To increase the level of challenge and intrigue, she also added a 'red herring' in the form of a picture of the front cover of a similar book (also featuring a girl and a tiger) and challenged pupils to see if they could spot this.

To make this technique manageable with a whole class, Debora began by asking the pupils to form a circle so that they could look at the pictures together before exploring them closely in smaller groups. The children were all able to order the pictures and to spot the red herring. They were very engaged by the activity, and their close attention to the pictures meant they were able to explain why the red herring was not a picture from the original story.

The teaching assistant (TA) was able to use the stepping stones again in the following lessons to prepare pupils for their writing tasks. Pupils were asked to find, and then stand next to, the picture that represented the beginning of the story and to talk descriptively about that picture prior to writing about it.

> Using different colours to denote different levels of challenge or task type.

Being able to observe which particular stepping stones the pupils find most difficult highlights where responsive teaching is called for. After the activity, display the problematic stepping stones as a visible reminder for pupils that this will be the focus of a targeted reteach.

Stumbling Blocks. Use large cardboard boxes to physically represent stumbling blocks. Stress the fact that genuine learning will be challenging, with many difficulties along the way. Each time a Stepping Stone activity – or any other learning activity – proves to be difficult, work with the pupils to distil the main issues and write these on the outer faces of the box. At appropriate moments, have pupils roll these like a die and discuss ways to address the points and 'get over' the stumbling block. The exaggerated size of the boxes and physical movement is a deliberately theatrical technique to highlight the significance of the metaphor and aid memorability.

360 Degree Flip. This innovative approach helps pupils to engage with key information but in a very memorable and active way, by repeating it several times with increasing independence.

> Begin by inviting the class to stand up and face the front of the room.

> Give a piece of key information and challenge the pupils simply to remember what you have just said.

> Then walk to one side of the classroom and ask your class to pivot 90 degrees to face you. Repeat the piece of key information and ask the pupils to repeat what you have said.

> Next, move to the back of the classroom and again ask the class to turn to face you. This time repeat the previous information but accompany it with an

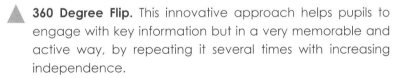 Responsive teaching ● Oracy and 'word wealth' ● Collaborative learning

appropriate action. Again, ask the pupils to repeat your words and copy the action.

> Walk to the other side of the classroom and have everyone turn to face you. This time don't say the words. Silently model the action, asking pupils to copy you but to repeat the verbal information as they do so.

> Finally, as you return, and your class rotates, to the starting position, remain silent and still. Indicate that you want pupils to say the words and do the action independently from memory.

> Use subsequent lessons to check how well the information has been retained by randomly selecting pupils and challenging them to repeat the words whilst the rest of the class perform the accompanying action.

Learning Arena. Clear a space to represent a learning arena ready for a gladiatorial activity. Encourage pupils to participate by asking, 'Who wants to step in and see if they can defeat the questions from the spectators?' This is a powerful way to cultivate growth mindsets by encouraging risk-taking. It does not have to involve pupils acting as lone gladiators; small groups work equally well.

Scaling Up. Use the floor space to allow pupils to access the most challenging concepts or content in a magnified way. This can also be a good opportunity to physically reposition yourself more as a guide on the side rather than leading from the front. Set up a large-scale activity in which pupils are working collaboratively and thereby appreciating the

benefits of using each other as a learning resource. Because the learning is more immersive, experiential and larger than normal, this is an ideal strategy to use when aiming for more profound understanding and retention. Variations could include:

> **A Giant Inductive Grid.** Pupils can 'walk the talk' by making and verbalising connections in what is essentially a performance space or learning arena. Establish that entering this space confers the right and authority to explore and express ideas speculatively using appropriate language – for example, 'could be ...', 'might mean ...', etc. Also, establish a 'climate of allies' so that everyone in the group is responsible for exploring and clarifying concepts.

> **A Giant Blockbusters Grid.** Set up a grid of tessellating hexagon tiles with a letter written on each one. Small teams compete to have their nominated player be the first to cross the grid by stepping on a tile and answering a question posed by the other team. To increase the difficulty, the answer must start with the letter on the tile. The questions could be generated in advance or thought up on the spot. You could also include additional rules – for example, help can be given by all the team/a different person each time, a time limit, a penalty/backward step if the team fails to answer, etc.

On a Roll. Move the furniture to reveal a space on the floor large enough to unfurl long rolls of paper – again, we'd recommend wallpaper for this. Invite pupils to gather around

Case study: The Dearne ALC

On a roll with learning

We saw a great example of On a Roll in a Year 9 geography lesson. The class had started their GCSE course and in this particular lesson they were all comfortably lying or sitting on the floor around a long, wide roll of paper. It was interesting to observe the quality of collaborative discussion and see the way in which some of the pupils were using mini-whiteboards to refine their thinking before adding their ideas to the roll. Their teacher, Rebecca, commented on how impressed she was with the enthusiastic way in which the pupils were all working together. She said that this was a great technique as, apart from clarifying and revising their knowledge, pupils now had an invaluable resource that they could easily and frequently come back to.

Comments from pupils summed up their reaction and thoughts:

'It's better than just sitting down. It's a more fun way to revise. I think this way will help us to remember because we enjoy it because we create it ourselves.'

'We feel a lot better being closer to each other and we can choose how we do it. I think teachers should put them up around the faculty so others can see and learn from them.'

'It's more fun because you can all talk to each other about it. In a normal lesson, we do more copying. This is more practical and you remember it better.'

and work collaboratively to cover the paper with representations of their current learning in a style of their choice. Without tables and chairs, pupils are literally in and amongst their learning. Providing notepads, mini-whiteboards or similar gives the pupils an opportunity to try out ideas and discuss them with others before transferring onto the roll itself. Explain that if there are any elements they cannot remember, they should first use each other as a resource and then refer back to their books if necessary. Observing exactly what pupils are checking in their books provides feedback as to which aspects may need checking or reteaching.

⬡ **Story Sheets.** This technique makes great use of a cheap white fabric sheet, which can simply be spread out over the floor. It was developed by the photographer of this book, Jane Hewitt, and is a wonderful way for pupils to let their storytelling imaginations loose and to become physically immersed in their learning.[2] Use marker pens and place newspaper underneath the sheet to protect the floor from any possible seep through. Encourage pupils to create their own location for the story setting, such as outer space, a forest, a town, etc. To stretch them, introduce extra elements which they need to discuss and portray. Some of the ideas we particularly liked included:

❯ Adding the historical aspects of a town.

❯ Depicting appropriate styles of monuments and buildings.

❯ Exploring potential tensions (the river next to the zoo was about to flood ...).

❯ Reacting to disasters (a fire, an invasion of giant insects, etc.).

The main advantage of using this technique to develop storytelling is the mental and physical freedom encouraged by the large scale, and by the positioning of pupils next to each other whilst working on the floor. In addition, fabric sheets are cheap and durable; they can be rolled or folded without tearing and are easily repositioned.

---

2 If you want to find Jane on Twitter, she is @janeh271.

⬤ Metacognition and self-regulated learning ❙ Emotional engagement ▲ Retrieval and revision

Big Circle, Little Circles. For the Big Circle, begin by seating the whole class in a large circle on the floor. Explain that the empty space in front of them is their learning arena and is very important. Next, display the main learning elements for the lesson within this circle. These could be:

> Key questions.

> Questions, separated from their answers.

> Key terms, separated from their definitions.

> Chopped-up sentences and the accompanying punctuation.

> The steps in a process, arranged out of sequence.

A rule of thumb here would be to use this highly visual and memorable strategy in order to teach particularly challenging or significant curricular content, such as place value in maths or speech marks in English (as we will see in the case study that follows). Secondary examples could include applying the correct steps when expanding double brackets in algebra or sequencing and developing a point, evidence, explanation (PEE) paragraph in English. The idea is to make all the elements as large and exaggerated as possible and to involve pupils by inviting them to step into the circle to physically move the learning around, explaining what they are doing as they do so.

Now for the Little Circles. Using hula hoops, or similar, organise the class into smaller groups on the floor. Their physical closeness is important here as they should literally be 'shoulder to shoulder, knee to knee'. Fill the hoops with tasks related to the Big Circle activity, but differentiated according to learning needs and targets. The idea is for the pupils to really focus on the challenge within their circle and to tackle it as a team. The well-known Spencer Kagan co-operative learning structure talking chips may be especially helpful here to ensure turn-taking (Kagan, 2001). Each pupil is given a limited number of chips or tokens which they must place in the centre of the table each time they wish to make a comment.

 Inner Circle Zone. For this technique, you will need a very large, very strong circular piece of elastic, much like the ones used many years ago in playground jumping or skipping games (you could buy elastic tape from a haberdashers and fasten the ends together – just make sure they are very secure). Move the furniture to the outside edges of the classroom and clear a space in the centre. Choose six pupils to stand inside the giant elastic band and stretch it into a roughly circular shape. Ask the rest of the class to stand in a large circle around the perimeter. Explain that each pupil needs to step into the exclusive 'inner circle' but they can only do this when they have correctly answered a question, or contributed to the discussion in some way. By challenging the class to get everyone inside as quickly as possible – and urging them to help each other with whispered clues – this becomes a very inclusive approach, which helps to underpin the climate of allies not judges that we are looking to create.

Case study: St Joseph's RC Primary

Lifting speech marks off the page

The focus for the Year 1 class was on the correct use of speech marks. This had been identified as a difficult concept for the age group, so the teachers, Claire and Siobhan, worked with us to trial a new approach. We decided to introduce them in a fun and memorable way and wanted to experiment with the idea of a learning arena, using Big Circle, Little Circles. We used direct speech from two stories the children were familiar with: 'Little Red Riding Hood' and 'Goldilocks and the Three Bears'. The lesson started with the children sitting in a circle. Claire and Siobhan had copies of speech from the stories in very large print so it was visible to all pupils.

"This chair is just right," said Goldilocks.

"Someone has been sitting in my chair!" cried baby bear.

"What big eyes you have," said Little Red Riding Hood.

"All the better to see you with," said Grandma.

However, the sentences and punctuation were all jumbled up. As a clue, the speech was in blue and the speaker in red and there were plenty of extra speech marks for pupils to use. The class referred to the opening and closing marks as 66 and 99.[3] Claire and Siobhan introduced an element of random selection by rolling a die to determine who

---

3 You may notice that we've used single quote marks throughout this publication but have used double here as this is the way the children were taught this content.

would enter the learning arena first to begin to position the sentence correctly. They counted backward or forward from a child depending on the number landed on. This resulted in all the children remaining engaged as they didn't know when the direction would change. The first child had to choose the correct opening speech mark (66). The second child chose the words spoken. The third child chose where the speech closed (99). Finally, the fourth child chose the speaker. This process continued until all the examples were completed.

The next task involved using hula hoops to form the Little Circles. This mimicked the large learning arena but also supported the transition of pupils into small groups. The hoops themselves made the children enthusiastic about the challenge ahead. The children worked in groups of four to do the same task but with different examples. At this age turn-taking can be difficult, so the teachers introduced the additional element of talking chips. This meant that each child had two turns to match the speaker to the speech, and place the speech marks correctly. If a child in the group was wrong, their peers were encouraged to use SWAN feedback (about strengths, weaknesses and next steps, as we saw in Critique Circuit in Chapter 1) to help them.

For the plenary, Claire and Siobhan had four examples of direct speech: three WASOLLs and only one WAGOLL. The children were invited to 'roam the room', looking at all four options before standing beside the one they thought was

the WAGOLL – this is another example of a GAS activity. They had been told beforehand that a teacher would 'cold call' a random child to explain their position, so everyone needed to think carefully about where they stood.

The children were very excited about the inclusion of hula hoops. The resulting learning was fun and Claire and Siobhan felt that the class remembered how to use speech marks because of this. Big Circle, Little Circles had been a new way to keep focus in the classroom and to enable every child to see and participate in the lesson, they said. They also commented that they believed it was a good way to aid the transition between early years and Key Stage 1, when children move from play-based learning to more formal settings. Claire and Siobhan said they had been able to use the carpet area to teach in a fun way and make use of all the other available space in the classroom. The large visuals used in the Big Circle on the carpet supported learning and the hula hoops focused the children in a smaller space for independent learning. Comments from the pupils summed up their feelings about the learning experience:

'It was fun and exciting!'

'Going back to the learning arena helped me with my work at the table.'

'It helped me to see the speech marks better, and using the dice to move backward and forward around the learning arena was fun.'

Tap the Talent. Ensure that pupils' movements around the room are as purposeful and dynamic as possible by challenging them to speak to as many people as possible in a set amount of time to trade ideas. This activity draws upon the pupils' varied skill sets, perspectives and dispositions, and has the added benefit of developing interpersonal skills and strengthening the sense of community within the classroom.

Guided Tours. This fantastic approach has long been favoured by drama teachers but can be used in any area of the curriculum. Begin by grouping pupils into pairs labelled A and B. Next, display an image that only those labelled A can see. Each pupil A then physically guides their partner, pupil B, who has their eyes closed, around the room. They must be careful to look after their partner and ensure that they come to no harm. As pupil A guides their partner around the room they describe the world that they want pupil B to see in their imaginations. With their words, they illustrate the landscape, the temperature, the aromas, etc. using the most precise and imaginative vocabulary possible. Next, challenge pupil B to draw what has been described before reversing roles and repeating with a different image.

This technique is incredibly useful in helping pupils to scrutinise the image on display whilst engaging in both an imaginary and physical journey through it. We have seen this used brilliantly to explore settings in stories, landscapes in geography and even to walk through the circulatory system in GCSE PE theory.

Fully Immersed. How about creating a truly immersive space by dimming the lights and projecting an image onto the floor for pupils to access and work on collaboratively? We know that a lot of schools are now moving away from using projectors in favour of LED touchscreens, so, rather than throwing the old projector out, how about checking if it could be repurposed and used vertically to project onto the floor? Some schools have taken this idea further by investing in the technology to effectively turn a section of floor space into an interactive whiteboard to further engage their pupils by enriching the sensory learning experience.

And What Else?

> ....

> ....

> ....

> ....

> ....

> ....

> ....

> ....

> ....

> ....

> ....

> ....

> ....

Chapter 4

ZONING: ONE CLASSROOM, ENDLESS POSSIBILITIES

In this chapter

We consider how the classroom can be reconfigured to create discrete zones which, by their very nature, help to encourage autonomous, exploratory learning experiences as pupils move between them. An added benefit is that these different zones help busy teachers to differentiate and intervene more effectively because they are working with smaller groups of pupils at any one time.

Sound familiar?

In the introduction, we mentioned that it is fundamentally beneficial for pupils' engagement if they can 'experience the finite classroom space in an almost infinite number of ways'. Teachers will also find zoning within the classroom useful in their endeavours to support the progress of individuals. Whilst whole-class teaching is common and powerful, the simple fact remains that, often, we need to work in a targeted way with smaller groups of pupils to unpick trickier aspects of learning. One-to-one tuition ranks highly as an effective strategy (see Hattie, 2008, and EEF Teaching and Learning Toolkit[1]) but is tremendously expensive and difficult to facilitate within typical classroom practice. However, establishing zones in the way described here not only allows teachers to get much closer to the learning of groups of pupils,

it has the added advantage that pupils can – and will – differentiate themselves according to needs and interests, allowing the teacher to see at a glance where their input and expertise is most needed.

In addition, by introducing different zones into the classroom we can further exploit the key principles of choice and challenge. Certainly, one of the great joys of the early years classroom is continuous provision which allows children to move freely through different areas. In early years settings, pupils are likely to encounter home corners, dressing-up corners, construction zones and water areas to name but a few. Crucially, at least some of these zones will be temporary with the layout, tending to change regularly in response to the learning content and how the teacher wants to deliver this. What is striking to observe in such classrooms is the sheer delight on the faces of the children as they navigate their way independently around their environment, especially when they encounter a new zone within their usual space. Awe and wonder abound along with plenty of physical movement as pupils lead their own learning.

However, as pupils progress through primary and secondary school, much of the spirit of continuous provision is lost – as we touched on in Chapter 3. Primary classrooms may still feature a reading corner or craft area but tend to become more standardised and traditional in their layout. Again, we'd do well to question why this is. Are pupils less motivated by variety, choice and movement as they get older? Or might it be the case

---

1 See https://educationendowmentfoundation.org.uk/evidence-summaries/teaching-learning-toolkit/one-to-one-tuition/.

⬤ Metacognition and self-regulated learning │ Emotional engagement ▲ Retrieval and revision

that teachers feel a sense of pressure increasing with the age of their pupils, leading to less creativity and freedom in classroom design? Perhaps rethinking, and then reorganising, the classroom as a whole feels like too much unnecessary work, particularly in a climate of accountability, targets and curriculum coverage.

So what needs to happen?

We believe that it can be highly beneficial to think about zoning any classroom, whatever the age of the learners. This allows a busy teacher to:

❯ Easily set up differentiated tasks and groupings and target support to those who need it most.

❯ Harness pupils' natural desire for movement rather than striving to suppress it.

❯ Use wall- or ceiling-mounted signs or labels to signpost and foreground some of the more abstract or complex aspects of learning by linking them to specific areas of the classroom – for example, the impossible corner, the reflective zone, etc.

Design the most responsive classroom possible

Perhaps most crucially, zoning is a very effective way to differentiate. By introducing different areas and choices, teachers can cater for the diverse needs of all their pupils more effectively. Furthermore, physical areas such as the Magpie Me and the Inward/Outward Classroom zones (both introduced in the Practical Techniques section in this chapter) allow the teacher to use a different approach by 'rooting' them in one place for a given time period, requiring the pupils to step into that zone when they need support. Not only does this help busy teachers to work more efficiently, it actively nurtures pupils' independent learning skills.

Offer choice and challenge

By chunking and dividing the whole classroom into designated areas we can provide further opportunities to engage and motivate by offering pupils carefully orchestrated choice and challenge. Later we'll see a really inspiring example from Adam's Year 10 maths lesson at The Dearne ALC. Obviously this freedom can be balanced with the flexibility to introduce more structure and support for any pupils who might find too much choice daunting.

● Metacognition and self-regulated learning ⏐ Emotional engagement ▲ Retrieval and revision

This allows teachers to retain something of the spirit of continuous provision and, what's more, it is easy to do. Of course novelty can be engaging, but this is not novelty merely for the sake of it, nor an opportunity for 'playtime'. Imagine the possibilities offered by:

❯ The research corner – complete with a range of suitable digital and non-digital resources to support pupils in conducting independent research.

❯ The recording corner – featuring sound tins, tablets or similar recording devices which pupils can use to distil and edit the essence of their thinking.

❯ The problem-solving corner – with a daily dilemma or two that will really get pupils thinking.

❯ The curiosity corner – featuring intriguing images, cryptic clues, puzzles or partial answers.

❯ The Prove It Place – detailed in the Practical Techniques section.

❯ The making corner – featuring a range of hands-on resources which pupils can use to demonstrate their learning in alternative ways.

❯ The impossible corner – detailed in the Practical Techniques section.

❯ The quiet zone – for individual thinking and working. All these suggestions would benefit all pupils, but this might be particularly helpful as a calmer area for pupils with SEND.

❯ The reading corner – perhaps with a tepee to settle down quietly in, or an inviting seating or lounging space.

Perhaps different types of lighting could be used to help distinguish the zones by creating an appropriate mood and signalling expectation through ambience – for example:

❯ Safe, battery-powered candles – to read by or to create a relaxed atmosphere.

❯ Spotlights – for focusing attention on a problem or challenge.

❯ Coloured lights – blue for 'blue sky' thinking and reflection, purple for progress zones, etc.

Recent studies asserted that lighting with different correlated color temperatures (CCTs) has profound effects on both the physical and mental conditions of humans.

(Choi and Suk, 2016)

You may find it useful to use removable tape – for example, masking tape – to physically set out areas for specific, differentiated, floor-based challenges. Having the tape in place means the furniture can quickly be moved to one side and the floor activities resumed whenever appropriate.

Weight the zones according to your curriculum priorities

It's up to teachers to use their skill to decide how to weight and resource the zones, dependent upon where the 'knottiest' parts of the learning are. For example, you may choose to have several zones devoted to the same challenging concept or skill. In each of these zones the pupils would engage with the same concept but in different ways – for example, younger pupils might kinaesthetically practise counting on using counters in one zone and then tackle some paper-based paired counting challenges in another. For pupils in a Key Stage 3 English lesson, poetic techniques could be explored using a mix-and-match activity in one corner and a choral reading or dramatic interpretation in another.

Create a classroom that best prepares pupils for real life

In the 2015 PISA tests, the UK ranked fifteenth amongst participating countries for collaborative problem-solving (see Ward, 2017): a skill which needs to be actively encouraged and cultivated in a range of ways. The creation of separate zones, together with opportunities to work collaboratively with different groups, is an effective way to encourage crucial exploratory thinking.

A systematic review of evidence across all phases of education identified the most effective learning environments and conditions which promoted the development of creative thinking and problem-solving skills and which were seen to impact on pupil attainment (Davies et al., 2013).

Amongst its findings the report stated that the classroom:

›   Should be conducive to being used flexibly to promote creativity. However, a note of caution is that some pupils, particularly those whose home life does not necessarily facilitate study, can find themselves alienated by too much flexibility.

›   Should encourage a sense of space and openness, enabling pupils to move around and make use of different areas to support the growth of ideas.

By being flexible learners – moving from zone to zone within a classroom, which itself flexes and shifts – we help our pupils to become more comfortable with the notion of change and to adapt to different ways of working, albeit on a small scale. As we are often reminded, relentless change is likely to characterise the learning future for all our young people. As stated in the popular YouTube video 'Shift happens', we are preparing them for jobs that do not yet exist using technologies that have not yet been invented.[2] As teachers, when we set up this kind of fluid classroom with its different zones, we are using the physical environment to model our own willingness to embrace change as well as providing opportunities for the pupils to explore and learn in different settings.

Customise your classroom

Ultimately, much of the joy of zoning lies in the creative possibilities it offers to teachers. What kinds of zones would best suit your philosophy and style of teaching? Where possible, involve the pupils in co-constructing the different zones: where and how do they think they might learn best? These zones and areas can be as temporary or as permanent as you wish: try to focus on embracing the concept of a 'fluid' classroom. It is also important to note that, on occasions, you may well choose to link zones to challenges that are very deliberately determined and teacher-directed.

Principles to underpin your practice

›   Choice and challenge are effective motivators for pupils.

›   Setting up zones within the classroom allows you to operate as a flexible and responsive teacher, able to support

---

2 Agility Consulting and Training, Shift happens 2018 ACT [video] (29 May 2018). Available at: https://www.youtube.com/watch?v=bRthSsFFI7Y.

the differing needs of your pupils more effectively by working with different groups in different ways.

> Science suggests an association between movement and increased learning gains. Moving whilst learning means an increase of oxygen to the brain, as well as increased mental alertness (see Jensen, 2005).

> Life is characterised by a relentless pace of change that many people find challenging. A classroom that shifts and changes regularly is a useful training ground for real life.

Practical techniques

Unexpected zones

These zones are specifically designed to heighten emotional engagement and anticipation and can be adapted to suit learners of all ages.

Locked Up Learning. Place a large cage in the centre of the classroom labelled with warnings such as 'Danger', 'Caution: may contain challenges' and 'Do not touch'. Fill the cage with a selection of texts and artefacts relating to your topic and explain that the contents are 'banned'. Exploit the excitement and intrigue by not allowing the pupils to engage with these … yet! You could use a large cardboard box if you're not able to find a cage, but you'll want to leave this part-open so pupils can get just a glimpse of the contents – an essential part of building the sense of anticipation and speculation.

Mystery Materials. Move the furniture to the edges of the classroom and place a table loaded with tantalising objects, materials, a big question, etc. in the centre, covered with a sheet. As colours and textures can carry very different meanings, you may want to think about the colour of the sheet and the mood or image you wish to connote. Do you want one layer or more? For example, you could use a blank sheet and one printed with hieroglyphics, maths or science symbols, nature images, etc. By varying the colour or style of the sheets you are also creating a series of reference points and memory markers. This comes into play when you ask questions like, 'What was under the green sheet last term?' to reactivate prior learning. The key thing here is that the table of stimuli – rather than the teacher – is the focal point and effectively 'leading' the learning. Invite the pupils to stand around the table to:

> Predict what might be concealed.

> Sneak a peek.

> Touch and guess.

> Talk about how they are feeling.

You could make this an even more profound experience by dimming or changing the lighting, as discussed in the introduction to this chapter – perhaps using a spotlight, torch, lamp or coloured bulb. You may also want to add

a soundtrack – for example, a particular piece of music, percussion rhythms or a voice-over – and possibly scents as appropriate. We all know how powerful smell can be in evoking particular memories.

Next, think about the big reveal and how the experience will be built on. This could be done in a variety of ways – for example:

> **Slowly or Quickly.** Reveal inch by inch or very suddenly – using voice or sound to enhance the dramatic build-up. For example, the theme from *Jaws* would be an effective piece of music to use.

> **Ready, Steady, Look.** On the count of three, pupils each take a hold of the edge of the sheet and send it up like a parachute, revealing what's underneath only temporarily. You could then incorporate Kim's Game, the memory game in which pupils have to recall and describe the objects on the table, once the sheet has settled back into place.

Follow Your Symbol. As pupils enter the classroom, issue them with stickers featuring random words or symbols. Don't explain what these mean. Instead, use them to build intrigue. When appropriate, simply point pupils in the direction of the zone that corresponds to their sticker. Ensuring that the zones are self-explanatory, or contain minimal instructions, kick-starts the collaborative discussion.

Under Wraps. Drape different-coloured blankets or sheets over the tables to denote different zones. Make this even more engaging by concealing a range of different activities and prompts under the material on each table. Urge groups to tackle the blanket challenges as stealthily as possible in order that the hidden objects remain a mystery for their classmates, as they will subsequently rotate around the zones to take on a new challenge.

Make It Your Own. An easy way to incorporate a more game-like approach is to adopt an overarching theme for your environment. This is another ideal opportunity for you to put your own creative stamp onto your classroom and is also very emotionally engaging for the learners. No two teachers are the same and no two classrooms should be. Pick a theme or analogy and design your zones around its component parts – for example:

> A racing circuit with pit stops and chicanes.

> The Grand National with Becher's Brook, the home straight, etc.

> A mountain climb with a final ascent, safe passage, etc.

Think about how you could represent these aspects physically within your classroom and how pupils would be moving between, and acting differently within, them.

■ Responsive teaching   ◆ Oracy and 'word wealth'   ● Collaborative learning

● Metacognition and self-regulated learning | Emotional engagement ▲ Retrieval and revision

Follow Your Quest. Emulate features of online gaming by setting up a quest or treasure hunt using the whole-school environment. An element of competitiveness could be encouraged as pupils race to complete the quest first. Pupils could receive their personalised, differentiated assignments in a variety of ways – for example, on a scroll, as a personal text or video message, in a top-secret envelope, etc. The main idea is that the pupils will be directed to engage with a sequence of increasingly difficult challenges, puzzles or codes that are concealed around the whole-school environment – for example, under a table, inside a library book, in a corridor display, etc. The expectation here is that the challenges are read, acted upon and covertly placed back for other pupils to discover.

Language zones

Talk Tally. This is a really useful way of encouraging pupils to engage with key vocabulary. Display focus words for the lesson or unit of work as a tally chart, with space for the pupils to add their names and the date at the side. When pupils prove that they can use a word correctly they can add their name to the tally chart. This can become quite motivating as pupils compete to add their name alongside all of the words. Encourage the class to spot-check their understanding in subsequent lessons by choosing a name and asking the individual to explain the word.

Case study: Codsall Middle School

Get on board

Here the teacher, Ruth, trialled a Talk Tally in her maths lessons. The zone was situated to one side of the classroom and updated by the adults as the class successfully used new words during the unit of work. The idea was to encourage pupils to engage more with key vocabulary, as this had been identified as a whole-school priority. It had proven to be a stumbling block as pupils were often failing to see the links between core subjects. Each time a pupil used a mathematical term from the Talk Tally correctly, one of the adults would record their name and praise the pupil publicly.

Pupils had been made aware in the initial lesson that the Talk Tally would remain there for the whole unit, with a daily focus on words which had not been explored or discussed fully within previous lessons. Plenary time was used effectively to ensure that each individual pupil was aware of their focus words for the following day. It did not take long before the pupils began to be quite competitive in their desire to use the vocabulary correctly and get their name alongside each word on the chart.

Claim the Connective. Use plastic wallets to display cards featuring connective words or phrases, colour-coded to denote their different purposes – for example, comparing, contradicting, adding to a point, qualifying, etc. Encourage pupils to go and claim the card when they have successfully used the word or phrase. Record this in a similar way to the Talk Tally technique. Alternatively, you could add a more game-like element by having groups of pupils select examples from the display wallets and place them in the centre of the table. Pupils can grab them when they use them and add them to their individual pile. Who has managed to gather the biggest selection or use the most unusual ones?

Choice and challenge zones

Self-Selection. Set up your classroom with different tasks and styles of activities for pupils to opt into. Stress that there is no such thing as a wrong selection. Choice is a great motivator and this approach echoes all that is positive about continuous provision in early years settings. However, it can be tailored as appropriate for older children with increased levels of challenge, the expectation of task-completion and ownership of time management.

Tantalising Trays. This is an alternative, intriguing approach to extension tasks. Stock a number of trays with different prompts and conceal them ready to use later. Contents could include visual clues, pictures, objects or even cryptic messages. An ideal storing place for these might be underneath the table

used as the focal point of the lesson. When you judge that pupils are ready for an extension activity, invite them to pull out one of the mystery trays to tackle and choose the physical area where they would like to work.

Question Conundrums. Try introducing a range of zones specifically designed to prepare pupils to answer questions more effectively. Examples could include:

> The research zone.

> The discussion zone.

> The brainstorming zone.

Invite pupils to opt into their preferred zone in order to get ready to answer a 'big question'. As it is thought that the average wait time following a teacher asking a question is less than three seconds, this strategy would do much to improve the quality and depth of pupil responses (Rowe, 1987). Increase the level of challenge and accountability for all pupils by asking, 'What can you show or tell me that proves you chose the right zone?'

Pupils could then enter a question generating zone where they formulate as many options as possible prior to ranking and refining them and selecting one to answer.

Wandering and Wondering. Place a selection of questions, prompts or other stimuli on tables around the room. Provide each pupil with some sticky notes and invite them to visit each prompt in their own time and in any order. Stress

● Metacognition and self-regulated learning | Emotional engagement ▲ Retrieval and revision

that they should not talk to anyone else but concentrate on generating their personal responses on the sticky notes before placing these alongside the stimuli. Notes could take the form of short answers, further questions, initial thoughts or maybe even emojis or other basic symbols for younger learners.

The silent aspect is important here, lending a meditative and thoughtful feel to the exercise. As pupils become more adept at this they can then be encouraged to respond to their peers' contributions as well the original stimulus, this time using a different-coloured sticky note or pen for clarity.

Ever More Challenging. Create zones based around higher-order thinking skills or perhaps the SOLO Taxonomy stages (see Biggs and Collis, 1982):

1   **Stage 1: Prestructural.** You can question yourself and identify what you do not yet know and need to find out.

2   **Stage 2: Unistructural.** You can identify one idea about a topic and articulate it.

3   **Stage 3: Multistructural.** You are able to pick out several ideas but these are typically unrelated to each other.

4   **Stage 4: Relational.** As you begin to master the complexity of the topic you can connect several ideas together.

5   **Stage 5: Extended abstract.** You can begin to work at a higher level of abstraction and generalise concepts to

a new topic or area. You are also now able to create new ideas based on your mastery of the subject.

Inviting pupils to work through these zones at their own pace provides a fantastic opportunity for the teacher to observe how they are physically progressing through the stages, allowing them to check for understanding, respond and intervene as and when appropriate.

Pose the Impossible. Pose an 'unsolvable' problem or challenging conundrum – much like the one featured in the film *Good Will Hunting* – for all pupils to see and ponder. Establish that this is an open invitation to tinker and have a go. Setting up a permanent impossible area, complete with laminated paper or mini-whiteboards encourages experimentation with, and reforming of, ideas over time. Clues and next-step prompts can always be added at strategic moments. If a version of your problem is placed in a main area of the school it automatically opens up the challenge and encourages collaboration, or competition, across different year groups.

Centre Stage. Think carefully about where you position yourself and your desk, as the teacher's desk is often perceived as the locus of control in the classroom. Consider moving the other furniture to the peripheries and placing your desk right in the centre: this will be the focus, but you won't. Instead, randomly select pairs of pupils to 'take over' the teacher's desk for the lesson or day. Once pupils are centre stage they can assume increasing responsibility – for example, by posing questions to the class (which may need to be provided or vetted by the teacher initially) and leading discussions.

Metacognition and self-regulated learning | Emotional engagement ▲ Retrieval and revision

Case study: The Dearne ALC

Maths that keeps you on your toes

In a Year 10 maths lesson, we saw how effectively the teacher, Adam, had used his time and creative energy to design his display areas as a series of zones. The classroom set-up very clearly reflected his personal philosophy, as well as showcasing the dynamics of how teaching and learning worked here. The pupils were well used to the fact that, in this classroom, maths learning was collaborative, speculative and very active. It was interesting to see just how seamlessly pupils moved between working on their assignments at tables in the centre of the room and the zones at the sides.

Once pupils had demonstrated good progress against the main lesson objective they could then attempt one of several challenging 'stretch' activities. This linked to a very innovative approach, the Roll and Stretch Zone, where pupils threw giant dice in order to determine which challenge they undertook. This technique introduced an element of randomness and unpredictability – rather than teacher-direction – and seemed incredibly popular with the pupils. Furthermore, it meant that they would all ultimately encounter all of the stretch activities and could not remain in their 'safe spot'.

The other zones were also dedicated to providing differing degrees of challenge. The concept of challenge can have negative connotations – and maths, in particular, can be a subject in which pupils, and adults, may feel more unable and unwilling to attempt a problem. However, here the names used to designate the areas reinforced the positive and exciting aspect of challenging oneself. The message was most definitely that maths is fun!

Zones included:

> **The Stretch Wall.** Each of the four floor-to-ceiling cupboard doors held a different stretch activity, with space to post different tasks and for pupils to write their solutions.

> **The Creative Corner.** This contained two laminated pieces of A2 squared paper, with space to attach an appropriate challenge. In this lesson, it was to, 'Create a technical question from today's learning and include at least one error in your working for other pupils to identify.'

> **The Impossible Corner.** A permanent feature, this also used large, laminated pieces of squared paper, with changing challenging conundrums. Interestingly this zone had been framed using black and yellow hazard tape, but it was certainly not a 'no-go area'. This was a space that invited pupils to 'hazard' a suggestion and explore their thinking.

A key feature of all of these zones was the scale. Everything was enlarged and pupils were encouraged to write directly onto the A2 laminated paper or onto the cupboard doors using dry-wipe markers. Being away from the constraints of a piece of A4 paper or an exercise book allowed the pupils the freedom to 'be messy' in their working and exploratory and speculative in their thinking. Their physical positioning in the space also facilitated movement and collaboration. A couple of pupils summed up their thoughts about the lesson:

> 'It expands your learning because you have to think outside the box. Moving helps me remember.'

> 'It's amazing. It's really good because it gets you up on your feet and you can talk to other people about it.'

These displays were distinctive in that they did not contain the more usual prompts, such as informative and attractive maths posters or even key vocabulary lists. These were dynamic zones where the emphasis was firmly on the process of how learning happens – and on becoming a mathematician – not just on content to be absorbed.

Here, the classroom itself seemed to be 'doing the teaching'. Adam had been able to use his professional knowledge and creativity to focus on identifying priorities for his pupils' progress. This meant that during the lesson he could operate more at the edge of the learning, where he was primed and ready to respond as required by pupils in real time. By taking advantage of the whole learning space in this manner, he has observed a marked increase in the level of focus, self-challenge and motivation demonstrated by many pupils. Seeing their peers make rapid and sustained progress has actually motivated pupils to work at a faster pace.

Responsive zones

Suspended Success Criteria. Hang differentiated success criteria from different areas of the ceiling or display them prominently on the tables. Then invite pupils to stand by the criteria they need to address next. Alternatively, invite pupils to stand by the criteria they would welcome feedback or support with, either from the teacher or a peer. This is a great strategy for empowering pupils to identify their own targets for development and has the added benefit of generating organic and evolving pupil groupings as the learners cluster around common needs or misconceptions. From an assessment perspective, teachers can see at a glance the percentage of pupils flagging particular criteria as problematic and can deploy their resources and energy appropriately in response.

Magpie Models. Set aside a zone within the classroom where WAGOLLs, those models of great work, are displayed. Explain that pupils can enter the magpie zone to borrow key words, phrases and ideas if and when necessary. You can stipulate how many times pupils can enter and what they are allowed to borrow.

Check Mate. At appropriate times, learning partners move into this zone to peer assess each other's work against a specified set of routine criteria – for example, punctuation, spelling, labelling of diagrams, etc. – or using a section from a subject-specific assessment rubric. Laminating sets of different criteria allows pupils to select the most appropriate one to check against. A useful extra would be questions for pupils to ask when checking each other's work, such as, 'What were you proud of?', 'What would you do differently next time?', 'What is the main thing you have learned here?' This firmly reinforces these types of questions in the minds of the pupils asking them, ready for future self-reflection.

Coaching Conference. Establish different themed zones to allow the teacher to work with groups of pupils in different ways. Examples could include:

> The conference table – where the big ideas are debated.

> The team huddle – for talking tactics and collaborative planning.

> The coaching bench – where pupils gather to share ideas when they are in need of support.

Introduce the pupils to the different layouts and expected ways of working in each and encourage them to:

> Select which layout the classroom needs at any one time.

> Assist in rearranging the classroom, if needed. Some teachers use appropriate music to encourage efficient routines when doing this.

Rooted Teacher. Rather than dashing around your classroom trying to anticipate and respond to the many different needs of your pupils, plant yourself in a particular zone and explain that – like a tree – you are rooted to the spot and will not move. Instead, pupils will visit you there. Even if you remain at your usual desk, talk up the fact that this is now a distinctive zone with particular expectations that pupils must be conscious of. Variations could include:

> **Helpful Huddle.** A space that is readily available so you can extract a small group of pupils to work with in the lesson. The carpet area is an ideal space for this in a primary classroom. Within a secondary setting, set aside a table for this purpose or, if space is an issue, place some extra seats around the teacher's desk, so that pupils can 'come into conference' with you.

> **Magpie Me.** A designated zone where you sit and work on the same task as the pupils but in a larger way, perhaps using A3 paper and marker pens to aid visibility. You can either invite particular pupils to visit you in this zone or make yourself available as a resource for all pupils. Rather than copying from you directly, challenge pupils to watch you and memorise what you are doing before transferring elements into their own work. This is different from typical live modelling in the sense that it is ongoing; you may repeat the same task four or five times, but differently depending on which pupils come to observe you. You will automatically find yourself slowing down and perhaps providing commentary for pupils who are struggling. For able pupils visiting out of curiosity, you may just offer them a quick glance before turning over your work and encouraging them to persevere on their own.

> **Secret Challenge.** A separate but prominent zone within the classroom where the teacher invites pupils to come and tackle intriguing secret challenges. These can be written versions of the typical questions teachers use to probe and extend understanding. Alternatively, these could take the form of envelopes containing key terms with the challenge being for pupils to provide definitions, etc.

The Inward/Outward Classroom. This set-up allows individuals to work quietly or collaboratively depending on their needs. Place tables around the periphery of the classroom, chairs facing outwards, for pupils who want to work on tasks independently. The inward area facilitates support and might resemble a conference table or be set up in a small horseshoe

arrangement. This space could be used for teacher-led work, such as guided instruction, targeted reteaching and feedback. The idea of meeting at the conference table is powerful as it repositions the teacher in relation to the pupils: it is non-hierarchical and more discussion-based. Such a layout allows a different sort of interaction and many pupils get very excited by the idea of being in the discussion space or conference zone. Ensure you leave room to move around the space, allowing all pupils access to the teacher, regardless of where they have chosen to work. Having these two designated zones would also allow the teacher and the TA to swap roles and to differentiate more effectively.

The Permeable Classroom. This idea builds on the culture of teachers' collective responsibility and involves different zones across several classrooms, so you'll need to recruit some willing volunteers from your year group or department. Each teacher works with their own classes as usual from Monday to Thursday, then they get together to review and regroup the pupils ready for differentiated interventions on Fun/Phenomenal/Fabulous Fridays. The focus on Fridays is on providing highly targeted provision, including reteaching, extension or consolidation activities. It is exciting to consider what becomes possible when we think about zoning across the whole department or school, and not just within one classroom.

Colour-Coded Feedback. Introducing colour-coded zones within the classroom is especially helpful when providing differentiated feedback during dedicated improvement and reflection time (DIRT) activities. For example, 'If I gave you a

Case study: Codsall Middle School

Intriguing in-class interventions

In this hands-on, investigative maths lesson with Year 5, the teacher, Ruth, was keen to support the pupils – many of whom found maths difficult and lacked confidence – more effectively. Prior to the lesson, she and the TAs had thought carefully about how to support the pupils, whilst at the same time encouraging them to be more resilient and independent when tackling their maths challenges. With this focus in mind, they prepared a list of questions and prompts for the two TAs to use to promote deeper learning. These included:

> 'Can you explain to me …?'

> 'Watch me doing this: am I doing it right or wrong?'

This approach worked well and allowed the TAs to move around the classroom to engage the pupils as and when appropriate using challenges and their own WASOLLs to demonstrate how to improve. Crucially, this allowed Ruth to think about how she could best use herself as a resource. She commented: 'Typically when I am walking around the class-room looking "available", pupils will swamp me with hands up and demands for help, even if they do not actually need it!'

In this lesson, she wanted to be more strategic and decided to set up a Secret Challenge. As the lesson unfolded, she quietly retreated to a simple-looking secret challenge zone by the whiteboard and observed how the learning was unfolding from her seat. She decided when pupils were ready to engage with this zone – either because they needed some extra help or an additional challenge – and began to call them over one pair at a time.

When the pairs entered the zone they were given a sealed envelope containing a secret challenge. Ruth deliberately used the idea of concealment and mystery to create a sense of intrigue and excitement, which was noticeable with other pupils saying things like, 'Don't spoil it by telling me what's in it – I want to wait for my turn to find out.'

Each of the envelopes was differentiated in advance according to the school's bronze, silver, gold system. However, Ruth didn't want pupils to feel dispirited if they had a bronze challenge so she drew shapes on the envelopes rather than showing the difference more overtly with colour-coding. She also told the pupils that they could come back and request a more difficult challenge once they'd successfully completed their original one; reaffirming the expectation that they would indeed rise to the challenge.

It was a very energetic lesson in which the pupils interacted with each other and discussed their work more than they had done previously. They were excited about their secret challenges and were very enthusiastic about attempting extra extension tasks. Ruth and the TAs felt they were working together more effectively to empower pupils towards the common goal of progress. Ruth felt that she had been able to view the learning from a different perspective – quite literally – and as such could intervene much more effectively. She also commented that their relationship as a class seemed to have grown greatly, concluding that the supportive and collaborative environment had encouraged the pupils to take risks which were fundamentally important in helping them to develop a growth mindset in maths.

pink dot as feedback in your book, come and join the pink table for your DIRT task.' More on this and other innovative feedback strategies can be found on Claire's blog.[3]

Progress zones

Prove It Place. This is an area where pupils can go to work on developing their 'mastery masterpieces': pieces of work that they have developed and refined over time. One teacher had put up a big sign which said, 'The difference between proving and improving is *I'm* ...' This put the focus firmly on the pupils taking responsibility for recognising and demonstrating progress over time through continued attempts to refine their work. This is a place for pupils to choose how they want to consolidate their own learning and take it to the next stage by presenting key information in a creative format. Ideas could include:

›   A quirky visual representation – the class could even vote for the most memorable one.

›   A tweet – a character-limit sharpens thinking and develops the crucial skill of summarising.

›   An elevator pitch – a succinct verbal description that explains the idea and can be easily understood by listeners.

›   A mime or rap. We saw a great example of this when a group of boys in a lower-achieving science class were enlisted to help the teacher come up with a memorable way of presenting key information about wavelengths. They were so keen they worked on it in their own time and delivered an amazing performance the following week.

›   A narrative retelling in a different style – perhaps a sports commentary or a story for pre-school children; think *Horrible Histories* and let your collective creativity run.

Pupil Portfolios. Set aside a designated zone in the classroom – or in a more public area like the hall or corridor – to house portfolios of pupils' work. Give this area status and encourage pupils to regularly visit to update their portfolios. As pupils are responsible for collating and highlighting their own achievements, this approach combines metacognition with celebration. An e-portfolio could work in the same way; however, even in this digital age, the more traditional, physical version still has much to offer in terms of celebrating pupil progress in a highly visible manner. The following variations are particularly powerful:

›   **Progress Portrait.** Set up a gallery of clear plastic folders – or photo frames if you've got the space and resources – and explain to pupils that this is their space where they can display the piece of work that they are

---

3 https://www.clairegadsby.com/blog/.

currently most proud of, i.e. their WOMBOLLs. This may be a written piece but could equally be a photograph of them demonstrating something practical. Ideally, this would be annotated to show exactly what they are pleased with and why. Empower and encourage pupils to regularly update their progress portrait so that it represents the current pinnacle of their personal achievement: their personal best. This is what we like to describe as 'weeding and feeding' your WOMBOLLs.

These stand-out celebration pieces not only make a great addition to the display culture but are brilliant for parents' evenings when parents can literally walk through their child's learning journey, with the child acting as a guide on the side. This would be even more effective if the current celebration piece was sitting in front of previous WOMBOLLs to show progress over time.

› **Progress Pull Out.** Use concertina plastic wallets that can be extended to show multiple drafts, or the genesis and journey, of a finished piece of work. This places the emphasis firmly on seeing progress as a process over time, involving a series of connected iterations. Alternatively, this could be folded to position the first and final draft side by side. These could be used to support pupils in the metacognitive process of reflecting on and consolidating their own learning and also to teach each other.

› **Personal Power Profiles.** Support pupils to create profiles that indicate their own unique areas of expertise. This can include interests and talents that have been developed outside of school – for example, skills with different types of technology, music, sports, etc. These profiles could be kept in a physical folder, displayed in a gallery or stored electronically – perhaps with accompanying videos of the pupils talking about their 'personal power'. These experts can then be used as research sources, consultants or mini-teachers by anyone who wants to find out more about their expertise.

Independence zones

› **Enable Table.** These function as repositories of resources for pupils to use before turning to the teacher. When pupils are struggling, encourage them to help themselves to items on the enable table. You may already have created such an area, stocking it with the usual learning aids – for example, dictionaries, thesauruses, pencils, calculators, Numicon, etc. However, we think there is room for even more creativity, such as:

› Including a range of visual organiser templates – for example, spider diagrams, affinity diagrams, mind maps, Venn diagrams, fish-bone diagrams, cycle-maps, etc.

› Using tablets to record the most significant teaching episodes in your lesson, such as a demonstration of an experiment or modelling how to write a paragraph. In essence, try to anticipate the most complex aspects of the process – and where pupils are likely to ask you to repeat the instruction – and record them. Place the tablet on the enable table and invite pupils to replay as and when necessary in order to avoid repeating yourself. Conserve your energy for trying other ways to move learners forward. Keep an eye on which pupils need to use the resources the most and intervene as necessary.

> Including multisensory support, such as a mystery prop bag full of text snippets or artefacts that might help to stimulate and develop pupils' thinking around a concept.

> Ensuring pupils are able to access learning that they may have missed – for example, 'Help yourself to last week's teacher-notes'. If you have used an interactive whiteboard during the lesson, you could take some screenshots and print out several copies. These could be placed in plastic wallets and displayed in an accessible place. This could be really useful if a pupil has missed a lesson, especially if a learning buddy or ambassador is assigned to discuss the content with them.

Earn It and Learn It. Use of the enable table can be incentivised and energised by incorporating an element of competition. Organise your class into groups, giving each one the same amount of counters in the form of tokens, points, fake money, etc. Explain that certain sources of knowledge in the classroom, such as helping each other and access to the enable table, are 'free'. Next, introduce the idea that other sources,

such as the teacher, are very 'expensive' – costing a certain number of tokens, points, money, etc. each time. You may choose to offer a discounted rate for a yes/no answer depending on how hard your class negotiates. Sometimes, merely responding with, 'Are you sure you want to use up a token by asking me this?' is enough to get the pupil to rethink independently. You could wear a jokey, pupil-made badge – perhaps something along the lines of 'Big Boss' – to remind them that you are the last port of call.

During the group task, circulate around the classroom, commenting loudly on the effective use of enablers and rewarding this with extra counters. Maintain momentum by introducing a league table where the groups' totals are tracked over time. This has proven to be a highly effective technique for keeping motivation high – particularly if combined with sporting terminology, such as promotion and relegation zones, to add a bit more interest.

Clue Corner. In a prominent position within the classroom, set out piles of cards containing helpful prompts or clues to support pupils in their learning. Perhaps try colour-coding these to denote the amount of information supplied, getting pupils to think about whether they just need a nudge in the right direction or a more substantial insight. Encourage pupils to physically move into the clue corner when they need help getting unstuck – perhaps with the stipulation that they should only do this after they have worked through the 4B Strategy. When you're stuck, check the following:

> Boards – whiteboard, display boards, etc.

> Books – your exercise book, textbooks and research resources.

> Brain – take a moment to think again. Perhaps set up a quiet, reflective 'thinking it through' area to support pupils and to demonstrably acknowledge the value in taking time out to reflect on learning.

> Buddy – in the form of learning partners, learning ambassadors, champions, experts, etc.

Give One, Take One. Develop the Clue Corner by creating the expectation that, if pupils take a card, they must write their own example – covering an aspect of the learning they are confident with – that can then be used to help other learners.

Expertise Area. Here, pupils take on the mantle of the expert and become ambassadors or mini-teachers. You could allocate specific times and spaces for the ambassadors to be accessed by other pupils. Alternatively, you could establish the understanding that they are an available resource and can be approached at any time during the topic. You could give them badges to declare their expertise: 'I feel like an expert in …', 'I am now ready for you to ask me about …', 'I asked a really good question today about …' or 'I am a learning ambassador for …' If the pupil wears the badge outside your classroom, other adults and pupils can ask them about it as well, so the significance is further increased and the benefit extended. Pupils can also decide on an appropriate VIP who they would like to visit to explain how their learning has developed. This could be the head teacher or another adult, but could also be a pupil, perhaps from a different class, to emphasise the fact that *everyone* in the school is important, not just the grown-ups. Have your pupils come up with a way of recording who has visited whom.

Teaching Takeover. Routinely involve pupils in the actual delivery of the lesson. This could be in the form of a presentation of a key learning point, a homework assignment, a prepared plenary, etc. Build in the expectation that these should be interactive sessions with questions and challenges flowing both ways – from the designated 'teachers' to the rest of the class and vice versa.

Variations on this idea might include:

> **Teach the Teddies.** Or a suitably 'mature' variation for older pupils. Set up a designated area as a mini classroom in which pupils are actively encouraged to mimic teaching in order to consolidate what they have learned. Other pupils could video, feed back or join in.

> **Teach It with Tech.** Pupils research a particular aspect of a new unit of work and use technology to present their findings. They could utilise the interactive whiteboard, video, animation (paper slide, plasticine stop-motion or a more elaborate form), podcasts, etc. This could be a great way to share the expertise of pupils who are more knowledgeable about various types of technology. Their digital lessons could then be shared on the school website, played on a welcome screen in the entrance foyer for parents and visitors to see, etc. This could be developed further by the pupils presenting and leading discussions about both the content covered in their lesson and the technology they used – for example, at assemblies or parents' evenings. They could even be designated 'tech experts', giving short tutorials on how to use that particular technological tool.

> **Review and Redesign.** Ask pupils to work in small groups to redesign a particular lesson that you have taught them and will be teaching to another class in future. What would they change? How would they make it better?

Pick a Card. Set up a small quiet area where individuals can work to solve increasingly difficult challenges. Create a series of cards with varying degrees of challenge and make these available for pupils to select from at any time. Create a code to indicate the level of difficulty – for example, this could be along the lines of bronze, silver, gold or mild, warm, red hot. The challenges could be linked to current or previous learning and vary in the type of response required. Alternatively, they could be a range of brain-teaser or mind-stretcher puzzles, which are not necessarily curriculum-based. Include a variety of puzzles to address different skills – for example, visual, spatial, logical reasoning, code-breaker, number, word and language puzzles. Pupils could earn rewards – such as badges, stickers or points – as they progress through the levels of challenge towards becoming a challenge champ. Another idea could be for pupils to keep a personal reflective log and record not only which challenges they attempted but also how they felt when tackling different ones. This could include an annotated selfie showing how they felt when they achieved something tricky. Cue the celebratory fist-pump, perhaps?

Creation Station. Designate an area of your classroom where your pupils can work collaboratively to create a challenging question, task or puzzle for others to attempt. This could also be uploaded to the school website or shared via social media so that pupils are encouraged to work on it outside of school. Challenge your pupils to devise a game that could be used to teach something they have recently learned to pupils in a different class. These could include customised traditional games, completely original ones of their own design, or existing commercial digital games. Pupils may surprise you by coming up with suggestions, which you may not have even heard of, that are related to the learning and will really grab their peers' interest. The availability of design tools and open competitions for creating digital games may mean that some pupils have had experience of this already and will relish the opportunity to explore it further in the classroom.

Case study: Codsall Middle School

Moving *and* thinking circuits

During a PE lesson the teacher, Alex, combined Circuit Training with a stepping stone challenge. He'd differentiated the stepping stones brilliantly according to the school's bronze, silver, gold system, and made them incrementally more difficult. Each stepping stone challenge prepared pupils for the next circuit training zone using anagrams, visual clues, questions, etc.

The lesson was focused on the effects of exercise and each station involved the students performing a practical activity. To make the transitions between those activities more meaningful and challenging, Alex used the stepping stones to get students thinking and talking about what processes were taking place in their bodies. This was a great, diagnostic way to see which groups needed intervention and which groups needed challenging further. Whilst this activity obviously works well in a PE practical lesson, it could also be used to good effect in PE theory lessons, or indeed any other subject, simply by replacing the physical activities for table-based ones.

Across the Barricades. Use a line of chairs to create a barrier down the middle of your classroom, thus forming two halves. Divide the class into two teams and set them a task. Ensure that each team is given different pieces of information that they will need to put together to complete the task. Pupils will need to meet at the barricade, where they must sit next to each other and trade their information. The problem-solving element, along with the active development of interpersonal and social skills makes this a really powerful technique.

Research Carousel. Set up different stations around your classroom with information about the topic presented in different forms – for example, videos, a variety of written sources, a selection of images, etc. Supply groups of pupils with key questions and challenges and let them move through the stations, giving them an appropriate amount of time in each to gather what they need. Stress the importance of teamwork and the expectation that, as a team, they must ensure that all of their members are confident that they've found the information and are ready to leave the station when the signal is given.

Circuit Training. This operates exactly like physical circuit training but instead of exercises the different stations (or tables) contain a variety of different learning activities. Pupils work in groups against the clock, rotating around at a given signal – perhaps this could be the blow of a whistle to reinforce the imagery. We've already touched on the merits of a circuit training approach in Ceiling Circuits in Chapter 2.

The stations should all be related to the same topic, but can include a variety of activities, for example:

> A series of questions to be answered.

> A talking chips discussion.

> A jigsaw to complete.

> A drama scene to improvise.

> A challenging cloze activity to fill in.

> A poor example of work to critique and improve – turn a WASOLL into a WAGOLL.

Enhance this still further by placing stepping stone challenges between the zones (see Chapter 3 for more information).

And What Else?

> ....

> ....

> ....

> ....

> ....

Conclusion:

THE LEGACY OF
THE LEARNING

As we said in the introduction, our aim in writing this book is to hopefully inspire you to reclaim your creativity. We want you to be able to take key findings from robust research and translate them into a range of engaging techniques that unlock the potential of various pedagogical approaches and the physical environment in order to make your classroom dynamically different.

We hope that you've made this book your own by adding extra ideas, comments and adaptations to some of the techniques. Moreover, we hope you've also started to note the impact that they are having on your pupils' engagement with their learning and also on your practice.

The legacy for your pupils

Most teachers say that they want what happens in their classroom to make a significant impact on all pupils, not just at the point of learning but also in the future. We want our pupils to develop a love of learning and become lifelong learners.

Although we haven't got a crystal ball to see exactly what the future will hold for today's young people, we can anticipate communication and problem-solving skills becoming increasingly valued in the 21st century. If we are committed to ensuring our pupils reach their potential in a rapidly changing world it becomes a moral imperative to provide truly meaningful experiences that cultivate these

skills. We must give our pupils the chance to get hands-on with projects that will develop the vital skills of communication, collaboration and creative, critical thinking in authentic contexts.

So, in this short concluding chapter, we first invite you to think about the ways in which your pupils' active learning can be enhanced further by utilising the wider school environment and collaborating even more extensively.

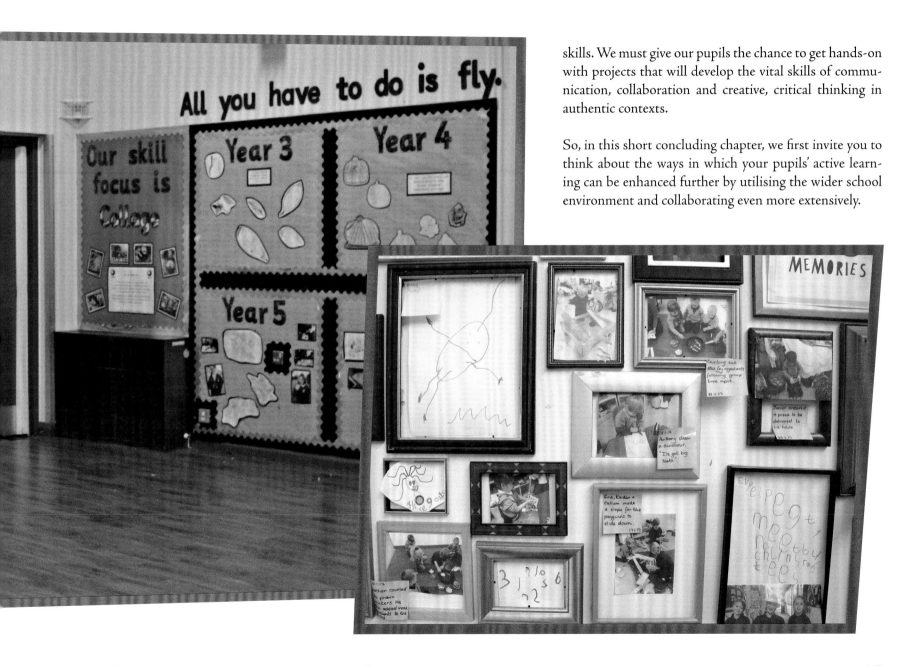

'I BLAME THE YOUNG MAN. HE OUGHT TO BE DEALT WITH VERY SEVERELY.'
'THE WHOLE STORY'S JUST A LOT OF MOONSHINE
mrs Birling

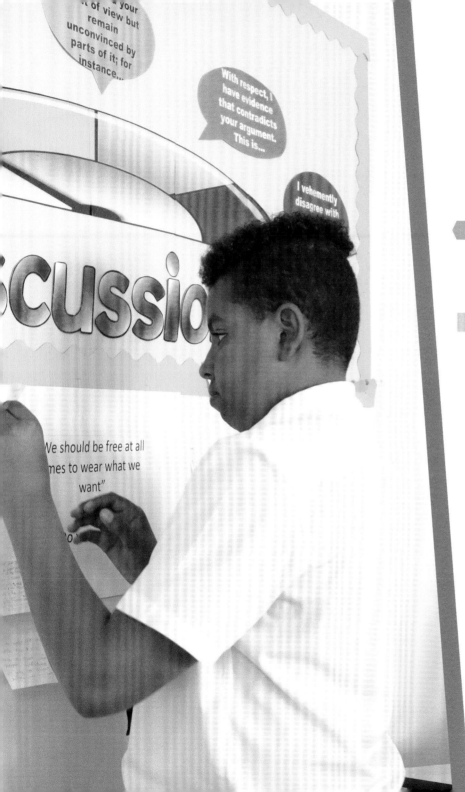

Practical techniques

Wider spaces and wider collaboration

Query It, QR It. Use QR codes in visible places, such as on windows or in the entrance foyer, so that parents and visitors can access aspects of current areas of learning. This could link to areas of extended research that parents might want to look at together with their child.

Corridor Content. Teachers can become quite protective of the allocated space outside their classrooms that is literally 'on display' to a wider audience, often using it to showcase attractive examples of work with clearly written labels. Yet so many people pass through the corridors on their journey around the school and, as such, this is fertile territory. So why not capitalise on this travel time by making it into a journey that exercises the mind as well as the legs? Promoting dynamic learning should be a whole-school drive and this shared space could be used to prioritise content and challenge in a way that creates the greatest good for the greatest number. Think carefully about your curricular and development targets as a school. For example, if you were looking to raise attainment in reading it would make sense to pepper the environment with stimulating, interactive content directly pertaining to this. Again the Pareto principle may be helpful in rationalising decisions about what deserves to be in this key territory.

Chalk It Up. Have a large chalkboard or whiteboard at the school gate or in the foyer. This can be used to explore a big question, a provocative statement or a real-life community or world issue. Invite pupils, parents and visitors to add their thinking. This can be a great opportunity to highlight the SMSC aspects of your curriculum in a truly collaborative way. Decide on an appropriate way to share this with an even wider audience – for example, via the school website, a blog, TED Talk-style presentations, etc.

Guru Gallery. Develop the idea of Personal Power Profiles from Chapter 4 but on a whole-school scale. Ideally, include the interests, areas of expertise and skills of the entire school staff, as well as the pupils. Create a gallery complete with photos which can be displayed somewhere prominent or accessed electronically. How about an augmented reality gallery with the portraits coming to life (Harry Potter style) to show promotional videos of the subject touting their talents? Apps like HP Reveal (formerly Aurasma) can be used for this purpose.

Create specific times – perhaps every half term – for special group projects that allow for creative thinking and sustained involvement. These could be cross-class, cross-year or even extended to family events. Create the expectation that a variety of Gurus should be called on, either as consultants or active group members. Once pupils leave the school, you can still retain their contributions to the Guru Gallery. Although ex-pupils will not be able to physically work along-side current ones during these projects, they could still pass on the benefit of their leaning legacy and expertise in the form of WAGOLLs, emails, video chats, etc.

Real Legacy Projects. These take the idea of an extended project even further as pupils will work on them throughout the year. As the name suggests, they provide collaborative opportunities for real engagement with *real* issues and bring the SMSC aspects of the curriculum well and truly to life in a visible, high-profile way.

At their heart, these projects will involve:

> Dealing with issues that are important for the wider community – whether this be on a school, local, national or global scale. These may come directly from areas of the curriculum or be suggested by the pupils themselves.

> Opportunities to collaborate with a range of people – this could be physically or virtually and could link with the Guru Gallery.

> Establishing what needs to be done to address the issues and then planning and carrying out an agreed course of action with regular progress checks.

> Choosing the appropriate media for presentation to a wider audience.

> Future-proofing the legacy so the project can be passed on to the next generation of pupils who will take on the responsibilities.

It's well worth reading the article 'Legacy projects: helping young people respond productively to the challenges of a changing world' (Beghetto, 2017) for further inspiration on designing key questions to explore through your projects. The author lays out an approach that involves pupils directly in analytical, creative, practical, wisdom-based and ethical thinking.

The legacy of your own professional learning

We know that the school culture can be a major factor in supporting or impeding teachers' creative practice. Teachers can be reluctant to veer away from traditional approaches, often citing an overcrowded curriculum, lack of time and the pressure of accountability within a high-stakes environment as some of the main barriers to developing more innovative techniques.

However, one of our mantras has always been, 'What we want for our pupils, we also want for our teachers' – i.e. regular opportunities to engage in creative thinking, speculative discussions and reflection within a climate of allies; regular opportunities to share and bounce ideas around; to take risks; to be able to refine and develop practice and impact on the practice of other people. In other words, a truly effective and reflective professional learning culture.

Therefore, we'd also like you to seriously think about how your own learning can be developed further and consider the implications for you and your colleagues as the lead learners in your school.

So, some questions to think about are:

> What will be the legacy of the new ideas you've tried?

> How do you model a creative and reflective attitude towards learning?

> How should other staff be involved?

> What is the vehicle for your own further learning?

> Anything else you can think of?

Practical techniques

Powerful Partners. Choose a close colleague to work with and establish a routine in which you identify a shared focus and trial the same, or a similar, technique to explore it. Hold each other accountable for keeping a short log, with photos if appropriate, of what you did and the impact you observed. Compare notes and decide on your next steps, or the next technique to try. If possible, talk to each other's pupils about what they thought of the strategy and how they felt. Gradually bring more partners into the process.

Networking. Use real-life or virtual networks across schools to share techniques you've been trying – for example, by attending TeachMeets or sharing insights on Twitter.

Staff Learning Wall. Make your progress visual. Take photos of the techniques in action and annotate with comments from you and your pupils about what went well. Put these up in a departmental or staffroom display space. A group of schools we worked with a few years ago covered a wall of the staffroom with giant jigsaw pieces that different teachers used to post their ideas. It became quite competitive; even more so when the deputy heads introduced a prize – often a bottle of wine or box of chocolates – for the most popular idea that week.

Assembly Ensemble. Once you have tried out and evaluated a few techniques with your pupils, enlist their support by asking them to put together a presentation to explain or demonstrate what has changed in the classroom and how they felt it impacted on their learning. Use assembly time for them to give their presentation to the rest of the school, year or key stage. When pupils explain the impact of the techniques on their learning it becomes a powerful catalyst for the further development of dynamically different classrooms.

Frequented Foyers. Use the entrance to the school to showcase videos of pupils explaining the impact on their learning, in a similar way to Assembly Ensemble. Once again, pupils are powerful advocates of the effectiveness of the techniques, and getting parents on board is another way to develop understanding and ensure long-lived impact.

Room Request. If the classroom is acknowledged as an interactive learning resource, with the physical environment actively used and frequently tweaked to challenge thinking, then this has an implication for room allocation and timetabling. Use team or departmental meetings to discuss collaborative approaches regarding the proactive use of the physical environment. This is particularly important if you share a classroom or are a 'nomadic' teacher.

Subject Specifics. Use subject meetings to really interrogate your specialist content and identify unique subject-specific priorities or particularly challenging concepts. Discuss how the physical environment can be used to address these, both within individual classrooms and in shared areas, and select techniques that will feed into this. Compare observations about effectiveness and impact within the department and across faculties if appropriate.

Lifelong Learning. Display photos or videos of staff on INSET sessions or courses, alongside comments about how they were feeling, what they were learning, what they will do differently based on what they've learned, etc. Make sure these are in a prominent place where pupils and visitors can see them. This shows how learning and reflection is a lifelong necessity, as well as conveying a sense of shared experience with pupils.

Performance Poem. Ask groups of teachers to use just a few words to complete the starter stem, 'Learning is …/A school is …' Then combine the ideas as a piece of poetry and film the teachers performing it. Upload the video to the school website or display on a screen in the foyer. How would the pupils' version compare if you asked them to do the same?

Shared Solutions. If particular whole-school issues or priorities are the subject of staff discussion, why not use a shared corridor space to identify these and invite others into the conversation? Include the positive aspects already in place as well as space to explore ideas and solutions. Attach a pad of sticky notes and a pen so staff, pupils and visitors can contribute their ideas. Alternatively, look at ways to employ a crowdsourcing approach via the school website, Twitter, etc.

And What Else? Let us know where your creativity takes you and your pupils (see page 163 for our contact details).

REFERENCES AND FURTHER READING

Adams, Richard (2018). Teachers in UK report growing 'vocabulary deficiency', *The Guardian* (19 April). Available at: https://www.theguardian.com/education/2018/apr/19/teachers-in-uk-report-growing-vocabulary-deficiency.

AFL (2009). Position Paper on Assessment for Learning from the Third International Conference on Assessment for Learning, 15–20 March, Dunedin, New Zealand. Available at: https://www.fairtest.org/sites/default/files/Assess-for-Learning-position-paper.pdf.

Agility Consulting and Training, Shift happens 2018 ACT [video] (29 May 2018) Available at: https://www.youtube.com/watch?v=bRthSsFFI7Y.

Banerjee, Robin (2010). *Social and Emotional Aspects of Learning in Schools: Contributions to Improving Attainment, Behaviour, and Attendance* (Brighton: University of Sussex). Available at: http://users.sussex.ac.uk/~robinb/SEALtracker.pdf.

Barrett, Peter, Yufan Zhang, Fay Davies and Lucinda Barrett (2015). *Clever Classrooms: Summary Report of the HEAD Project (Holistic Evidence and Design)* (Manchester: University of Salford). Available at: https://www.salford.ac.uk/cleverclassrooms/1503-Salford-Uni-Report-DIGITAL.pdf.

Beghetto, Ronald A. (2017). Legacy projects: helping young people respond productively to the challenges of a changing world, *Roeper Review* 39(3): 187–190.

Berger, Ron, Libby Woodfin and Anne Vilen (2016). *Learning That Lasts: Challenging, Engaging, and Empowering Students with Deeper Instruction* (San Francisco, CA: Jossey-Bass).

Biggs, John and Kevin Collis (1982). *Evaluating the Quality of Learning: The SOLO Taxonomy* (New York: Academic Press).

Bower, Bruce (2018). Huge 'word gap' holding back low-income children may not exist after all, *Science News* (4 September). Available at: https://www.sciencenews.org/article/word-gap-low-income-children-psychology-reproducibility.

Bowkett, Steve, Tim Harding, Trisha Lee and Roy Leighton (2007). *Success in the Creative Classroom: Using Past Wisdom to Inspire Excellence* (London: Bloomsbury Academic).

Bridge, Gillian (2016). *The Significance Delusion: Unlocking Our Thinking for Our Children's Future* (Carmarthen: Crown House Publishing).

Busch, Bradley and Edward Watson (2017). *Release Your Inner Drive: Everything You Need to Know About How to Get Good at Stuff* (Carmarthen: Crown House Publishing).

Choi, Kyungah and Hyeon-Jeong Suk (2016). Dynamic lighting system for the learning environment: performance of elementary students, *Optics Express* 24(10): A907–A916. Available at: https://www.osapublishing.org/oe/fulltext.cfm?uri=oe-24-10-A907&id=340246.

Csikszentmihalyi, Mihalyi (2002). *Flow: The Classic Work on How to Achieve Happiness* (London: Rider).

Davies, Dan, Divya Jindal-Snape, Chris Collier, Rebecca Digby, Penny Hay and Alan Howe (2013). Creative learning environments in education: a systematic literature review, *Thinking Skills and Creativity* 8: 80–91.

Dawes, Lyn (2018). Talk is for learning, *Oracy Cambridge* [blog] (7 April). Available at: https://oracycambridge. org/2018/04/07/talk-is-for-learning/.

Department for Education and Skills (2004). *Building Bulletin 98: Briefing Framework for Secondary School Projects* (London: Department for Education and Skills). Available at: http:// webarchive.nationalarchives.gov.uk/20130402164551/ https://www.education.gov.uk/publications/standard/ publicationDetail/Page1/BB-98.

Department for Education and Skills (2005). *Building Bulletin 99: Briefing Framework for Primary School Projects* (London: Department for Education and Skills). Available at: http:// webarchive.nationalarchives.gov.uk/20130402164554/ https://www.education.gov.uk/publications/standard/ publicationDetail/Page1/BB-99.

Dix, Paul (2017). Wristband peer feedback. In Isabella Wallace and Leah Kirkman (eds), *Best of the Best: Feedback* (Carmarthen: Crown House Publishing), pp. 45–50.

Dweck, Carol S. (2014). The power of yet [video], TEDxNorrköping (12 September). Available at: https://www. youtube.com/watch?reload=9&v=J-swZaKN2Ic.

Dweck, Carol S. (2017). *Mindset: Changing the Way You Think to Fulfil Your Potential* (London: Robinson).

Education Endowment Foundation (2018). Collaborative Learning: Teaching and Learning Toolkit (30 August). Available at: https://educationendowmentfoundation.org.uk/ pdf/generate/?u=https://educationendowmentfoundation. org.uk/pdf/toolkit/?id=152&t=Teaching%20and%20 Learning%20Toolkit&e=152&s=.

EL Education (2012). Austin's butterfly: building excellence in student work [video], *Vimeo* (9 March). Available at: https:// vimeo.com/38247060.

Fletcher, David and Mustafa Sarkar (2016). Mental fortitude training: an evidence-based approach to developing psychological resilience for sustained success, *Journal of Sport Psychology in Action* 7(3): 135–157.

Frey, Nancy, Douglas Fisher and Sandi Everlove (2009). *Productive Group Work: How to Engage Students, Build Teamwork, and Promote Understanding* (Alexandria, VA: Association for Curriculum and Development).

Griffith, Andy and Mark Burns (2012). *Engaging Learners* (Carmarthen: Crown House Publishing).

Hattie, John (2008). *Visible Learning: A Synthesis of Over 800 Meta-Analyses Relating to Achievement* (Abingdon: Routledge).

Jensen, Eric (2005). *Teaching with the Brain in Mind*, 2nd edn (Alexandria, VA: Association for Curriculum and Development).

Kagan, Spencer (2001). Kagan structures for emotional intelligence, *Kagan Online Magazine* (San Clemente, CA: Kagan Publishing). Available at: https://www. kaganonline.com/free_articles/dr_spencer_kagan/278/ Kagan-Structures-for-Emotional-Intelligence.

Koch, Richard (2017). *The 80/20 Principle: The Secret of Achieving More with Less* (London: Nicholas Brealey Publishing).

Leahy, Siobhan and Dylan Wiliam (2009). From teachers to schools: scaling up professional development for formative assessment. Presentation at the American Educational Research Association annual conference, 14 April, San Diego, USA. Transcript available at: https://www.dylanwiliam.org/Dylan_Wiliams_website/Papers.html.

Loftus, Jack (2011). Praising failure: James Dyson talks vacuum's 5,127 prototypes, *Gizmodo* (4 October). Available at: https://gizmodo.com/5790556/praising-failure-james-dyson-talks-vacuums-5127-prototypes.

McFall, Matthew (2013). *The Little Book of Awe and Wonder: A Cabinet of Curiosities* (Carmarthen: Independent Thinking Press).

Mercer, Neil (2003). The educational value of 'dialogic talk' in 'whole-class dialogue'. In *New Perspectives on Spoken English in the Classroom: Discussion Papers* (London: Qualifications and Curriculum Authority), pp. 73–76.

Moss, Stephen (2017). Half of Britain's prisoners are functionally illiterate. Can fellow inmates change that?, *The Guardian* (15 June). Available at: https://www.theguardian.com/inequality/2017/jun/15/reading-for-freedom-life-changing-scheme-dreamt-up-by-prison-pen-pals-shannon-trust-action-for-equity-award.

nasen (2015). *Supporting Pupils with Specific Learning Difficulties (Dyslexia) in Secondary Schools: A Quick Guide to Supporting the Needs of Pupils with Dyslexia* (Tamworth: nasen). Available at: http://www.nasen.org.uk/resources/resources.supporting-pupils-with-specific-learning-difficulties-spld.html.

Pink, Daniel (2010). *Drive: The Surprising Truth About What Motivates Us* (Edinburgh: Canongate Books).

Prensky, Marc (2010). *Teaching Digital Natives: Partnering for Real Learning* (Thousand Oaks, CA: Corwin).

Quigley, Alex (2018). *Closing the Vocabulary Gap* (Abingdon: Routledge).

Quigley, Alex, Daniel Muijs and Eleanor Stringer (2018). *Metacognition and Self-Regulated Learning: Guidance Report* (London: Education Endowment Foundation). Available at: https://educationendowmentfoundation.org.uk/public/files/Publications/Campaigns/Metacognition/EEF_Metacognition_and_self-regulated_learning.pdf.

Roberts, Hywel and Debra Kidd (2018). *Uncharted Territories: Adventures in Learning* (Carmarthen: Independent Thinking Press).

Robson, Kelsey and Sonia Mastrangelo (2017). Children's views of the learning environment: a study exploring the Reggio Emilia principle of the environment as the third teacher, *Journal of Childhood Studies* 42(4): 1–16. Available at: https://journals.uvic.ca/index.php/jcs/article/view/18100.

Rowe, Mary Budd (1987). Wait time: slowing down may be a way of speeding up, *American Educator* 11(1): 38–43.

Soderstrom, Nicholas C. and Robert A. Bjork (2013). Learning versus performance. In Dana S. Dunn (ed.), *Oxford Bibliographies*. Available at: http://www.oxfordbibliographies.com/view/document/obo-9780199828340/obo-9780199828340-0081.xml.

Stafford, Tom (2012). Why can smells unlock forgotten memories?, *BBC Future* [blog] (13 March). Available at: http://www.bbc.com/future/story/20120312-why-can-smells-unlock-memories.

The Prince's Trust (2017). *The Prince's Trust Macquarie Youth Index* (London: The Prince's Trust). Available at: https://www.princes-trust.org.uk/about-the-trust/news-views/the-princes-trust-2017-macquarie-youth-index-released-today.

Ward, Helen (2017). Pisa: UK does better than expected in collaborative problem-solving – rankings at a glance, *TES* (21 November). Available at: https://www.tes.com/news/pisa-uk-does-better-expected-collaborative-problem-solving-rankings-glance.

Wiliam, Dylan (2006). Assessment for learning: what, why and how. In Rebekah Oldroyd, *Excellence in Assessment: Assessment for Learning*. A supplement to the Cambridge Assessment Network Assessment for Learning Seminar held on 15 September 2006 in Cambridge, UK. (Cambridge: Cambridge Assessment Network), pp. 2–16.

Wiliam, Dylan and Paul Black (1990). *Inside the Black Box: Raising Standards through Classroom Assessment* (London: GL Assessment Ltd).

Williamson, Margaret and David Wilson (2012). *Kinetic Letters: Making Hand-Writing Easy for Everyone* (Winchester: Mole Press).

Wilson, Gary (2013). *Breaking through Barriers to Boys' Achievement: Developing a Caring Masculinity*, 2nd edn (London: Bloomsbury).

Wilson, Gary (2018). Boys will be … brilliant! Getting it right for boys in primary and secondary education. Keynote speech at the Engage and Support the Progress of Boys conference, Optimus Education, 13 June, London.

LIST OF STRATEGIES

● Metacognition and self-regulated learning | Emotional engagement ▲ Retrieval and revision
▦ Responsive teaching ⬟ Oracy and 'word wealth' ⬢ Collaborative learning

ABOUT THE AUTHORS

Author of the popular book *The Perfect Assessment for Learning*, Claire Gadsby is an educational consultant, trainer and keynote speaker with more than 20 years of experience in education who has worked with thousands of schools in the UK and internationally to raise achievement. Claire believes passionately in 'walking the talk' and regularly coaches teachers in the classroom to demonstrate innovative pedagogies. A leading expert on formative assessment, time-efficient feedback, literacy and reading, Claire strives to improve outcomes for all learners and to help teachers to work smarter not harder.

Email: info@clairegadsby.com

Twitter: @greatergadsby

Jan Evans is an education consultant with over 30 years' experience in education. She was the lead consultant in Oxfordshire for AfL and co-authored materials for the Secondary National Strategy. Her other specialist areas of expertise include: developing personal learning and thinking skills, promoting autonomous learning and developing interactive pedagogy. She has extensive experience of working with school leadership teams to develop strategic approaches to school improvement as well as leading a range of whole-school training programmes.

She regularly coaches teachers at all stages of their careers and is committed to helping them reclaim their creativity. She prides herself on being able to motivate teachers to develop innovative teaching and learning strategies through her enthusiastic, practical approach, coupled with a sense of humour.

Email: janet.evans27@gmail.com

Twitter: @ Janet_Evans27